# Alone But Not Lonely: Trekking Through Old Mother Wilderness

aarat

Published by aarat, 2024.

While every precaution has been taken in the preparation of this book, the publisher assumes no responsibility for errors or omissions, or for damages resulting from the use of the information contained herein.

ALONE BUT NOT LONELY: TREKKING THROUGH OLD MOTHER WILDERNESS

**First edition. April 17, 2024.**



ISBN: 979-8224044764

Written by aarat.

# Table of Contents

# Alone in the Wilderness

Chapter 1:

In the heart of a dense forest, far from the bustling streets and the noise of modern life, there resided an old woman known only as Old Mother Wilderness. Her weathered face bore the marks of time, etched with lines that spoke of countless seasons spent in solitude. Her eyes, deep and knowing, held the secrets of the wilderness, reflecting the wisdom of ages past.

Old Mother Wilderness was a figure of mystery and intrigue, a solitary soul who had chosen to make her home amidst the untamed beauty of the forest. She had wandered these woods for as long as she could remember, finding solace in the quiet whispers of the trees and the gentle rustle of leaves underfoot.

To those who ventured into the depths of the forest, she was a legend, a mysterious presence whispered about in hushed tones around campfires. Some said she was a guardian of the wilderness, while others believed her to be a wise woman with powers beyond mortal comprehension. But to Old Mother Wilderness herself, such labels mattered little. She was simply a part of the forest, as integral to its existence as the ancient trees that surrounded her.

In her solitude, she found peace. Away from the chaos and clamour of the outside world, she was free to roam the forest at her leisure, her only companions the birds that sang overhead and the animals that darted through the underbrush. Each day brought new discoveries, new wonders to behold in the ever-changing tapestry of the natural world.

And so, beneath the canopy of green that stretched endlessly overhead, Old Mother Wilderness lived out her days in quiet contentment. She had found her place in the world, a sanctuary far removed from the trappings of civilization's embrace. And as the seasons turned and the years passed by, she remained a steadfast presence in the heart of the forest, a living testament to the enduring power of solitude and the beauty of a life lived in harmony with the wilderness.

Despite the solitude, she found solace in the embrace of nature, where every rustle of the leaves and whisper of the wind spoke to her soul. Each day began with the soft symphony of the forest awakening around her, as birds greeted the dawn with their melodious songs and sunlight filtered through the canopy above.

As the first rays of sunlight pierced through the thick foliage, Old Mother Wilderness would emerge from her modest shelter, a simple cabin nestled among the ancient trees. Stepping outside, she would inhale deeply, savouring the crisp morning air that carried with it the earthy scent of damp soil and the sweet perfume of wildflowers.

With each step she took, the forest came alive around her. Squirrels scurried through the branches overhead, chattering excitedly as they gathered nuts and seeds for the day ahead. Deer grazed peacefully in sun-dappled clearings, their gentle eyes reflecting the tranquillity of the wilderness.

But it was the birdsong that truly filled Old Mother Wilderness's heart with joy. From the smallest warbler to the mighty eagle soaring high above, each bird added its voice to the chorus, creating a symphony of sound that echoed through the forest. Closing her eyes, she would listen intently, allowing the music of the natural world to wash over her like a gentle wave.

In those moments, she felt a profound connection to the land that surrounded her, a sense of belonging those transcended words. For here, in the heart of the forest, she was not alone. She was part of something greater – a vast tapestry of life woven together by the threads of existence itself.

And so, with each passing day, Old Mother Wilderness would immerse herself in the beauty of her surroundings, finding solace and comfort in the embrace of nature. For her, the forest was not just a place to live, but a sanctuary for the soul – a sacred space where the worries and cares of the world melted away, leaving only peace and tranquillity in their wake.

Old Mother Wilderness moved with the grace of one intimately familiar with her surroundings, her footsteps light upon the forest floor as she ventured forth to gather firewood or tend to her modest garden. Though her movements were slow and deliberate, there was a quiet strength in her demeanour, born of years spent navigating the rugged terrain of the wilderness.

With each step, she moved with purpose, her weathered hands deftly weaving through the undergrowth as she gathered fallen branches and dry leaves for kindling. Her eyes, sharp and keen, scanned the forest floor for signs of life – a footprint in the mud, a glimmer of movement amidst the shadows – ever vigilant to the subtle shifts of the natural world.

As she worked, the forest seemed to come alive around her, the trees whispering secrets in a language only she could understand. The gentle breeze carried with it the soft murmur of leaves, while the distant call of a lone wolf echoed through the trees. To Old Mother Wilderness, each sound was a message, a sign from the wilderness itself guiding her on her journey.

And though her body may have grown weary with age, her spirit remained as indomitable as ever. For beneath the surface of her weathered exterior lay a quiet strength – a resilience born of years spent facing the challenges of the wild. She had weathered storms and braved the depths of winter, emerging each time stronger and more determined than before.

For Old Mother Wilderness, the forest was not just her home, but her sanctuary – a place where she could be herself, free from the constraints of society and the expectations of others. Here, amidst the towering trees and the gentle babble of the stream, she found peace and purpose in the simple rhythms of nature's embrace.

And so, with each passing day, Old Mother Wilderness would venture forth into the heart of the forest, her footsteps echoing softly against the forest floor as she moved with grace and purpose. For her, there was no greater joy than to be immersed in the beauty of the wilderness, to feel the earth beneath her feet and the wind upon her face, knowing that she was exactly where she was meant to be.

As the seasons changed and the weather grew harsh, Old Mother Wilderness faced the elements with unwavering resilience. She hunted for her food, relying on her keen instincts and knowledge of the forest to sustain herself through the long winter months. Each day brought its own challenges, but she met them with a steadfast determination born of a lifetime spent in communion with the wild.

In the depths of winter, when the forest lay shrouded in a blanket of snow and ice, Old Mother Wilderness's survival skills were put to the test. With the streams frozen over and the ground buried beneath layers of frost, she had to rely on her wits and resourcefulness to procure food and shelter.

Venturing out into the cold, she would track the movements of the forest's inhabitants, following the telltale signs of their passing through the snow-covered landscape. With bow in hand and senses alert, she would stalk her prey with the patience of a hunter, waiting for the perfect moment to strike.

And when success came, as it inevitably did, Old Mother Wilderness would give thanks to the forest for providing her with sustenance. With practiced hands, she would skin and gut her quarry, wasting nothing and honouring the life that had been sacrificed so that she may live.

But hunting was not her only means of survival. In her cabin, nestled among the trees, she had cultivated a small garden where she grew vegetables and herbs to supplement her diet. Though the harsh winter months made gardening a challenge, she tended to her plants with care, nurturing them through the cold until the first signs of spring began to appear.

And so, as the seasons cycled through their endless dance, Old Mother Wilderness continued to thrive in her forest home. Though the challenges she faced were many, she met them with a resilience and determination that belied her years. For she knew that in the heart of the wilderness, there was no room for weakness – only strength, survival, and the enduring bond between humankind and the natural world.

And so, amidst the towering trees and meandering streams of her forest home, Old Mother Wilderness lived out her days in quiet solitude. Though the outside world remained a distant memory, she found fulfilment and purpose in the simple rhythms of nature's embrace. For her, the wilderness was not just a place of refuge, but a sanctuary where she could truly be herself, free from the constraints of society and the burdens of the modern world.

In the tranquil embrace of the forest, Old Mother Wilderness found a sense of belonging that she had never known elsewhere. Here, amidst the ancient trees and the gentle babble of the stream, she felt a connection to something greater than herself – a primal force that pulsed through the very heart of the wilderness, binding all living things in a delicate tapestry of existence.

Each day brought new wonders to behold – the vibrant colors of autumn leaves, the delicate blossoms of springtime flowers, the symphony of insects buzzing in the summer air. With each passing season, the forest revealed its secrets to her, teaching her the timeless lessons of patience, resilience, and respect for the natural world.

And though her life may have been solitary, it was never lonely. For in the company of the forest's inhabitants – the birds, the animals, the trees themselves – she found companionship and camaraderie of a different kind. They became her friends, her confidants, her family, sharing in the joys and sorrows of her everyday existence.

In the quiet moments of the evening, as the sun dipped below the horizon and the stars began to twinkle overhead, Old Mother Wilderness would sit by the fire, lost in thought. And as she gazed up at the vast expanse of the night sky, she felt a sense of peace wash over her – a deep-rooted certainty that she was exactly where she was meant to be.

For in the heart of the wilderness, amidst the towering trees and the gentle rustle of leaves, Old Mother Wilderness had found her home. And though her days may have been filled with solitude, they were also filled with purpose, meaning, and a profound sense of connection to the world around her.

# Memories of a Lifetime

Chapter 2:

Old Mother Wilderness rose with the dawn, the first rays of sunlight filtering through the canopy above and casting a golden hue upon the forest floor. As she set about her daily routine, memories of a lifetime flooded her mind, like sunlight breaking through the mist.

She recalled the days of her youth, when laughter echoed through the trees and love bloomed like wildflowers in the meadow. Her husband had been her steadfast companion, his laughter mingling with hers as they wandered hand in hand through the forest, their hearts intertwined like the roots of the ancient trees around them.

Though he was no longer by her side, his spirit lingered in every corner of their wilderness home, a silent presence that whispered of love and loss, of joys shared and sorrows endured. In the rustle of leaves and the babble of the nearby stream, she heard his voice, calling out to her from the depths of memory.

But even as she mourned his passing, Old Mother Wilderness found solace in the beauty of the world around her. For though her husband was gone, the love they had shared remained, a beacon of light that guided her through the darkness. And as she moved through the forest, her footsteps echoing softly against the forest floor, she carried his memory with her, a silent companion on her journey through life.

In the early days of their marriage, Old Mother Wilderness and her husband had been kindred spirits, bound together by a love that transcended time and space. They had ventured into the forest together, exploring its hidden nooks and crannies, discovering its secrets and marvelling at its beauty.

Hand in hand, they had wandered through the dense undergrowth, their laughter echoing through the trees like birdsong. They had marvelled at the majesty of towering redwoods and danced beneath the shimmering light of the moon. Each new discovery was a cause for celebration, a testament to the wonders of the natural world and the boundless love they shared.

Together, they had forged a life amidst the beauty of the wilderness, building their cabin from the ground up and tending to their garden with care. They had shared meals by the fire, stories by candlelight, and dreams beneath the stars. And as they lay entwined in each other's arms, they knew that they were exactly where they were meant to be – together, in the heart of the forest they called home.

Together, they had built their cabin from the ground up, using only the materials that the forest provided. Each log had been carefully selected, each stone placed with love and care. And as they worked side by side, their bond grew stronger, forged in the crucible of shared labor and shared dreams.

They had labored tirelessly, their hands calloused and their muscles sore, but their spirits undaunted. With each swing of the axe and each stroke of the saw, they had breathed life into their humble abode, infusing it with the warmth and love that had brought them together.

As the walls rose around them, they revelled in the sense of accomplishment that came with each new milestone. They had built their home with their own two hands, fashioning it from the very earth itself. And as they stood together beneath the completed roof, looking out over the forest that stretched endlessly before them, they knew that they had created something truly special – a sanctuary where their love could flourish and grow.

But it was not just the physical labor that bound them together – it was the shared dreams and aspirations that fuelled their efforts. They had envisioned a life of simplicity and harmony, a life lived in communion with the natural world. And as they worked together to bring those dreams to fruition, their bond grew stronger, cementing their commitment to each other and to the life they had chosen to build together.

But it was not just the physical labor that bound them together – it was the laughter they shared, the quiet moments of reflection, the stolen kisses beneath the stars. In each other's arms, they found solace and comfort, strength, and support, as they faced the challenges of life together.

Their days were filled with simple pleasures and shared joys. They would sit by the fire in the evenings, recounting tales of their adventures and dreams for the future. They would stroll hand in hand through the forest, their voices mingling with the rustle of leaves and the chirping of crickets. And when night fell, they would lie beneath the blanket of stars, lost in each other's embrace, as the world around them faded into darkness.

In those quiet moments, they found refuge from the cares of the world, their love a beacon of light that illuminated the darkness. They shared their hopes and fears, their triumphs, and disappointments, knowing that no matter what challenges lay ahead, they would face them together, hand in hand, heart to heart.

And as they gazed into each other's eyes, they saw not just the person before them, but the reflection of their own souls – bound together for eternity, united in love and devotion. For in each other's arms, they found the strength to weather any storm, the courage to chase any dream, the faith to believe that anything was possible as long as they were together.

Old Mother Wilderness smiled as she remembered those early days, the days of innocence and youth, when the world seemed full of endless possibilities. They had dreamed of a future filled with happiness and adventure, of growing old together amidst the beauty of the forest they called home.

In those days, their hearts had been filled with hope and excitement, their spirits buoyed by the promise of a life lived in harmony with nature. They had imagined themselves exploring every corner of the forest, discovering its hidden wonders and forging memories that would last a lifetime.

And though life had taken unexpected turns and their journey had been marked by trials and tribulations, their love had remained steadfast, a beacon of light that guided them through even the darkest of days. They had weathered storms and faced adversity, but through it all, their bond had only grown stronger, their love only deepened.

Now, as Old Mother Wilderness looked back on those early days, she felt a sense of gratitude wash over her – gratitude for the love they had shared, for the memories they had created, for the dreams they had dared to dream. And though her husband was no longer by her side, she knew that their love would endure, spanning the vast expanse of time and space, binding them together for all eternity.

But fate had other plans. As the years passed by, illness had claimed her husband, stealing him away from her before his time. Old Mother Wilderness had nursed him as best she could, but in the end, there was nothing she could do to save him. And so, she had been left alone, with nothing but memories to keep her company.

The loss had been devastating, a gaping hole torn in the fabric of her existence. For a time, she had felt adrift, lost in a sea of grief and sorrow. Her heart had cried out for him, longing for his touch, his laughter, his presence. But no matter how much she wished and prayed; he would never return to her side.

In the days that followed his passing, Old Mother Wilderness had felt as though the very essence of her being had been stripped away, leaving her hollow and empty. She had wandered through the forest like a ghost, her footsteps echoing against the trees like a dirge. Everywhere she looked, she saw reminders of him – in the cabin they had built together, in the garden they had tended with care, in the stars that shone brightly overhead.

But as the weeks turned into months and the months turned into years, Old Mother Wilderness began to find solace in the memories they had shared. Though her husband was gone, his spirit lived on in every corner of their wilderness home, a silent presence that whispered of love and loss, of joys shared and sorrows endured. And though she missed him with every fiber of her being, she knew that their love would endure, spanning the vast expanse of time and space, binding them together for all eternity.

In the aftermath of her husband's passing, Old Mother Wilderness had been consumed by grief. For a time, it had felt as though the world had lost all its color, all its vibrancy. But slowly, ever so slowly, she had begun to heal, finding solace in the familiar rhythms of the forest, in the beauty of the world around her.

At first, the pain had been all-consuming, a relentless ache that gnawed at her heart and soul. Everywhere she looked, she saw reminders of him – in the empty chair by the fire, in the silence that echoed through the cabin, in the empty space beside her in bed. It appears his absence filled every corner of their wilderness home, casting a shadow over everything she did.

But as the days turned into weeks and the weeks turned into months, Old Mother Wilderness began to find comfort in the simple rhythms of nature. She would rise with the sun each morning, greeting the day with a sense of quiet resolve. She would tend to her garden, coaxing life from the soil with gentle hands and a tender heart. And as she worked, she would lose herself in the beauty of the world around her, finding solace in the whisper of the wind through the trees, in the laughter of the nearby stream, in the rustle of leaves beneath her feet.

Slowly, ever so slowly, the pain began to ebb away, replaced by a sense of peace and acceptance. Though she would always carry her husband's memory with her, she knew that life must go on. And so, she turned her face to the sun and embraced each new day with a sense of quiet gratitude, knowing that even in the darkest of times, there was still beauty to be found in the world around her.

And though her husband was gone, his spirit lived on in every corner of their wilderness home. In the whisper of the wind through the trees, in the warmth of the fire crackling in the hearth, in the memories that filled her heart and soul. He was with her always, a guiding light in the darkness, a source of strength and comfort in times of need.

Old Mother Wilderness felt his presence everywhere she turned – in the soft rustle of leaves outside her window, in the flickering shadows cast by the fire, in the laughter of the birds as they danced through the air. Though he may have left this world, his spirit remained woven into the very fabric of their wilderness home, a silent presence that wrapped her in its embrace.

In moments of doubt and uncertainty, Old Mother Wilderness would close her eyes and reach out for him, feeling his presence surround her like a warm blanket. And in those moments, she would find the courage to face whatever challenges lay ahead, knowing that he was there beside her, guiding her every step of the way.

And though the ache of his absence would never truly fade, Old Mother Wilderness took comfort in the knowledge that their love was eternal – a bond that transcended time and space, uniting them across the vast expanse of the universe. For as long as she lived, he would live on in her heart, a beacon of light that illuminated even the darkest of days.

As Old Mother Wilderness reflected on the life she had shared with her husband, she felt a sense of gratitude wash over her – gratitude for the love they had shared, for the memories they had created, for the legacy they had left behind. And though he may have been gone, she knew that their love would endure, spanning the vast expanse of time and space, binding them together for all eternity.

In the quiet moments of the evening, as the sun dipped below the horizon and the stars began to twinkle overhead, Old Mother Wilderness would sit by the fire, lost in thought. And as she closed her eyes and listened to the gentle sounds of the forest around her, she felt her husband's presence beside her, his spirit shining brightly in the darkness.

She remembered the laughter they had shared, the dreams they had dared to dream, the love that had sustained them through even the darkest of days. And though he may have left this world, she knew that their bond was unbreakable – a thread woven through the fabric of the universe, connecting them across time and space.

And so, as she gazed up at the stars above, Old Mother Wilderness felt a sense of peace wash over her – a deep-rooted certainty that their love would endure, transcending the boundaries of mortality and reaching out into the infinite expanse of the cosmos. For as long as she lived, he would live on in her heart, a testament to the enduring power of love and the unbreakable bond that bound them together for all eternity.

And so, as the sun began to set on another day in the wilderness, Old Mother Wilderness sat by the fire, lost in thought. The crackling flames cast dancing shadows across the walls of her cabin, and the soft glow illuminated the worn features of her face. She closed her eyes and listened to the gentle sounds of the forest around her – the whisper of the wind through the trees, the distant call of a night bird, the rustle of leaves in the breeze.

In that moment of quiet reflection, she felt her husband's presence beside her, his spirit shining brightly in the darkness. It was as though he was sitting right there beside her, his hand resting gently on her shoulder, his voice a soothing murmur in her ear. And in that moment, she knew that she was never truly alone.

For though he may have passed from this world, his love remained as constant as the stars above. It wrapped around her like a warm embrace, filling her with a sense of peace and contentment. She could feel him guiding her, protecting her, loving her, until the end of time.

With a smile playing at the corners of her lips, Old Mother Wilderness opened her eyes and gazed into the fire. The flames danced and flickered, casting their warm light into the darkness of the cabin. And as she sat there, surrounded by the quiet beauty of the wilderness, she knew that no matter what the future held, she would always carry her husband's love with her – a light to guide her through even the darkest of nights.

# The Rhythms of Nature

Chapter 3:

In the heart of the wilderness, where the ancient trees whispered secrets to the wind and the babbling brooks sang melodies of old, Old Mother Wilderness lived in perfect harmony with the rhythms of nature. To her, every sunrise was a promise of new beginnings, a fresh canvas upon which the day's adventures would unfold. And with each sunset, she found solace in the quiet reflection of days gone by, in the gentle whispers of memories that danced on the evening breeze.

But it was not just the grand spectacle of dawn and dusk that captivated her – it was the small, simple moments that made up the tapestry of life in the wilderness. She reveled in the symphony of bird songs that greeted her each morning, their melodies a reminder of the beauty and abundance of the natural world. And as night fell, she marveled at the dance of fireflies, their soft glow illuminating the darkness like stars fallen to earth.

In the embrace of nature's symphony, Old Mother Wilderness found peace – a deep, abiding sense of contentment that filled her soul and lifted her spirit. For to her, the wilderness was not just a place to live, but a sanctuary, a refuge from the noise and chaos of the outside world. And in its quiet embrace, she found beauty in the simplest of things – in the rustle of leaves, in the ripple of water, in the gentle rhythm of life that pulsed through the forest like a heartbeat.

As dawn broke over the horizon, painting the sky with hues of pink and gold, Old Mother Wilderness greeted the new day with a sense of quiet anticipation. The forest came alive with the sounds of waking creatures – the chirping of birds, the rustle of small animals in the underbrush, the gentle babble of the nearby stream.

With each passing moment, the world around her stirred from its slumber, casting off the cloak of night and embracing the light of a new day. Old Mother Wilderness watched with a sense of wonder as the first rays of sunlight filtered through the trees, illuminating the forest in a golden glow.

It was a time of new beginnings, of fresh possibilities waiting to be discovered. And as she stood amidst the beauty of the wilderness, Old Mother Wilderness felt a surge of excitement coursing through her veins. For in the heart of the forest, anything was possible – and with each new day came the promise of adventure, of exploration, of endless discovery.

With each passing hour, the forest changed and evolved, a living, breathing entity that pulsed with the rhythm of life. Old Mother Wilderness moved through the landscape with a sense of reverence, her footsteps light upon the forest floor as she sought to become one with the natural world around her.

She marveled at the intricate dance of life that played out before her eyes – the delicate balance of predator and prey, of life and death, of growth and decay. Everywhere she looked, she saw evidence of the interconnectedness of all living things, each one playing its part in the grand tapestry of existence.

As she walked, she felt the pulse of the forest beneath her feet, the thrum of life that resonated through every leaf and blade of grass. She listened to the symphony of sounds that surrounded her – the rustle of leaves in the breeze, the chatter of squirrels in the treetops, the distant call of a lone wolf.

And with each step she took, Old Mother Wilderness felt herself drawn deeper into the heart of the wilderness, her senses alive with the sights and sounds of the natural world. For here, in this place of quiet beauty and untamed wildness, she felt truly alive – a part of something much larger and more mysterious than herself.

As the day wore on, she found herself drawn to the edge of a meandering stream, its clear waters sparkling in the sunlight. She knelt beside the bank, dipping her hand into the cool water and marveling at the feeling of connection it brought her. Here, in the embrace of nature, she felt at peace – a sense of belonging those transcended words.

And as she sat beside the stream, listening to the gentle rush of water over rocks, Old Mother Wilderness felt a profound sense of gratitude wash over her. For in this moment, surrounded by the beauty and majesty of the wilderness, she knew that she was exactly where she was meant to be – a part of the natural world, in perfect harmony with its rhythms and cycles.

In the heart of the wilderness, time seemed to slow and stretch, flowing like a river through the landscape. Old Mother Wilderness felt the ebb and flow of the seasons like a heartbeat, each one bringing its own unique beauty and challenges. She marveled at the delicate blossoms of spring, the lush greenery of summer, the fiery hues of autumn, and the quiet stillness of winter.

Spring was a time of rebirth and renewal when the forest burst forth in a riot of color and life. Old Mother Wilderness watched with delight as the first signs of spring appeared – the tender buds on the trees, the vibrant wildflowers carpeting the forest floor, the chorus of birdsong that filled the air. It was a time of new beginnings, of fresh growth, of the promise of warmer days to come.

As spring gave way to summer, the forest came alive with activity, teeming with life in every corner. Old Mother Wilderness reveled in the warmth of the sun on her skin, the cool shade of the trees overhead, the sweet scent of wildflowers carried on the breeze. She watched as the animals raised their young, as the plants reached for the sky, as life bloomed and flourished in every direction.

But as the days grew shorter and the nights grew colder, the forest began to change once again, heralding the arrival of autumn. Old Mother Wilderness watched as the leaves turned from green to gold, orange, and red, painting the landscape in a fiery palette of colors. She listened to the rustle of fallen leaves underfoot, the honking of geese overhead, the distant call of migrating birds as they made their way south. It was a time of transition, of letting go of the old and preparing for the new.

And when winter finally descended upon the forest, cloaking it in a blanket of snow and ice, Old Mother Wilderness found beauty even in the cold. She marveled at the intricate patterns of frost on the windowpanes, the shimmering crystals of snow that blanketed the ground, the hushed silence that enveloped the world like a soft embrace. It was a time of quiet reflection, of inner contemplation, of rest and renewal in preparation for the cycle to begin anew.

Through it all, Old Mother Wilderness remained steadfast in her love for the wilderness, finding beauty and wonder in every season, in every moment. For to her, the rhythms of nature were not just a part of life – they were life itself, a constant reminder of the interconnectedness of all living things and the beauty of the world in which we live.

But it was not just the changing seasons that captivated Old Mother Wilderness – it was the smaller, more subtle rhythms of nature that truly spoke to her soul. She watched with delight as the trees budded in spring, their leaves unfurling like delicate green flags in the breeze. She listened with wonder to the chorus of frogs that heralded the arrival of summer, their voices rising in a cacophony of sound that filled the night air.

In the quiet moments of the morning, she would stand at the edge of the forest, breathing in the sweet scent of pine and earth, feeling the gentle touch of the breeze on her skin. She would watch as the first rays of sunlight filtered through the trees, casting dappled patterns of light and shadow on the forest floor. And in those moments, she felt as though she were a part of something much larger than herself – a tiny piece of a vast, interconnected web of life.

As the days grew warmer and the nights grew longer, Old Mother Wilderness found herself drawn deeper into the heart of the wilderness, her senses alive with the sights and sounds of the natural world. She marveled at the delicate beauty of wildflowers blooming in the meadows, their petals swaying gently in the breeze. She listened to the buzzing of bees as they danced from flower to flower, pollinating plants and spreading life wherever they went.

And as the sun set on another day in the wilderness, Old Mother Wilderness would sit by the fire, lost in thought. She would listen to the night sounds – the hoot of an owl, the distant howl of a coyote, the rustle of small animals in the underbrush. And in those moments, she felt a sense of peace wash over her – a deep, abiding connection to the natural world that sustained her through even the darkest of nights.

For to Old Mother Wilderness, the rhythms of nature were not just a part of life – they were life itself, a constant reminder of the beauty and wonder of the world in which we live. And as she stood on the edge of the forest, surrounded by the sights and sounds of the wilderness, she knew that she was exactly where she was meant to be – at home, in the heart of nature.

AND AS THE DAYS GREW shorter and the nights longer, Old Mother Wilderness felt a sense of peace settle over the forest like a blanket of snow. She watched as the animals prepared for the long winter ahead, gathering food and finding shelter against the cold. And she too prepared, stocking her pantry with preserves and firewood, readying herself for the quiet months that lay ahead.

In the waning days of autumn, Old Mother Wilderness could feel the chill of winter creeping in, carrying with it the promise of snow and ice. She watched as the animals grew restless, their movements quickening as they scurried to gather the last of their provisions.

Squirrels busied themselves gathering nuts and seeds, while birds flocked to the feeders, eager to stock up on food before the snows came.

As the days grew colder, Old Mother Wilderness turned her attention to her own preparations for winter. She spent long hours in the kitchen, preserving fruits and vegetables from her garden, canning jams and pickles to see her through the lean months ahead. She gathered firewood from the forest, stacking it neatly beside the cabin to keep her warm during the long winter nights.

And as the first flakes of snow began to fall, Old Mother Wilderness felt a sense of satisfaction wash over her. She knew that she had done all she could to prepare for the coming winter, and now it was time to settle in and wait out the cold. She lit a fire in the hearth, watching as the flames danced and flickered, casting a warm glow throughout the cabin.

As the days grew shorter and the nights longer, Old Mother Wilderness found comfort in the quiet solitude of winter. She spent her days tending to her chores, knitting by the fire, and reflecting on the year gone by. And as the snow piled high outside her door, she felt a sense of peace settle over her – a deep, abiding contentment that came from knowing she was safe and warm in her wilderness home.

For to Old Mother Wilderness, winter was not just a season of cold and darkness – it was a time of quiet reflection, of inner contemplation, of rest and renewal in preparation for the cycle to begin anew. And as she sat by the fire, surrounded by the warmth and light of her cabin, she knew that she was exactly where she was meant to be – at home, in the heart of the wilderness.

But even in the depths of winter, when the world lay frozen and still, Old Mother Wilderness found beauty and wonder all around her. She marveled at the delicate patterns of frost on the windowpanes, the shimmering blanket of snow that covered the forest floor, the crisp, clean scent of the air.

As she stepped outside into the winter landscape, Old Mother Wilderness felt a sense of awe wash over her. The forest was transformed, draped in a cloak of white that sparkled in the sunlight. The trees stood silent and still, their branches heavy with snow, their outlines softened by the winter haze.

Everywhere she looked, she saw evidence of the magic of winter – the intricate patterns of frost that adorned the windowpanes, the delicate icicles that hung from the eaves, the hushed silence that enveloped the world like a soft blanket. And as she walked through the snow-covered landscape, Old Mother Wilderness felt a sense of peace settle over her – a quiet stillness that filled her with a deep sense of contentment.

In the heart of winter, Old Mother Wilderness found solace in the beauty of the natural world. She watched as the animals adapted to the cold, their fur thick and fluffy, their movements slow and deliberate. She listened to the sound of the wind as it whispered through the trees, the crackle of the fire as it burned in the hearth, the soft padding of her footsteps in the snow.

And as she stood beneath the clear, cold sky, Old Mother Wilderness felt a sense of gratitude wash over her – gratitude for the beauty and wonder of the world around her, for the peace and tranquility of the wilderness, for the rhythms of nature that sustained her through even the darkest of days.

For to Old Mother Wilderness, winter was not just a season of cold and darkness – it was a time of beauty and wonder, of stillness and reflection, of finding peace in the quiet solitude of the natural world. And as she stood amidst the snow-covered landscape, surrounded by the sights, and sounds of the wilderness, she knew that she was exactly where she was meant to be – at home, in the heart of nature.

And when spring finally came again, bursting forth in a riot of color and life, Old Mother Wilderness rejoiced in the renewal of the world around her. She watched as the flowers bloomed, the trees budded, and the animals emerged from their winter slumber, their hearts filled with the promise of new beginnings.

As the snow melted away and the days grew longer, the forest came alive with the vibrant energy of spring. Old Mother Wilderness marveled at the sight of delicate blossoms unfurling, their petals reaching eagerly towards the sun. She listened to the joyful chorus of birdsong that filled the air, as feathered creatures heralded the arrival of warmer days.

Everywhere she looked, she saw evidence of new life – tiny buds bursting forth from branches, tender shoots pushing their way through the soil, newborn animals taking their first tentative steps into the world. And as she walked through the forest, Old Mother Wilderness felt a sense of awe wash over her – a deep appreciation for the beauty and wonder of the natural world.

In the heart of spring, Old Mother Wilderness felt a renewed sense of hope and optimism. She watched as the world around her burst forth in a riot of color and life, each day bringing new surprises and delights. And as she stood amidst the beauty of the wilderness, surrounded by the sights, and sounds of the natural world, she knew that she was exactly where she was meant to be – at home, in the heart of nature.

For to Old Mother Wilderness, spring was not just a season of renewal – it was a time of rebirth, of growth, of endless possibility. And as she watched the world awaken from its winter slumber, she felt a sense of joy and gratitude wash over her – a deep, abiding appreciation for the beauty and wonder of the world in which we live.

In the heart of the wilderness, Old Mother Wilderness felt a deep connection to the natural world around her. She understood that she was but a small part of a larger whole, a single thread woven into the intricate tapestry of life. And though she may have been just one person, she knew that her actions had the power to shape the world around her – for better or for worse.

As she moved through the forest, Old Mother Wilderness did so with a sense of reverence and respect for all living things. She tread lightly upon the earth, leaving behind only the faintest of footprints as she went. She gathered only what she needed from the land, taking care to leave the rest for the creatures who called the wilderness home.

Old Mother Wilderness understood the delicate balance that existed in the natural world – the interconnectedness of all living things, the web of relationships that bound them together. She knew that every plant, every animal, every rock and stream had its place in the grand scheme of things, and that upsetting that balance could have far-reaching consequences.

And so, she lived her life with intention and mindfulness, striving to live in harmony with the rhythms of nature and to leave the world a little better than she found it. She planted trees, tended to her garden, and cared for the animals that crossed her path, knowing that each small act of kindness had the power to make a difference in the world.

For Old Mother Wilderness, the wilderness was not just a place to live – it was a way of life, a philosophy, a way of being in the world. And as she stood amidst the towering trees and meandering streams of her forest home, she knew that she was exactly where she was meant to be – at one with the natural world, in perfect harmony with its rhythms and cycles.

And so, she lived her life with a sense of mindfulness and reverence, striving to leave behind a legacy of harmony and balance. She treated the earth with respect, mindful of the impact her actions had on the delicate ecosystems that sustained life. She lived simply, mindful of the resources she consumed and the waste she produced.

Old Mother Wilderness believed in the importance of living in harmony with the natural world, of treading lightly upon the earth and leaving behind a minimal footprint. She practiced conservation and sustainability in all aspects of her life, from her daily habits to the way she managed her land.

She composted her food scraps, turning them into nutrient-rich soil to feed her garden. She collected rainwater to water her plants, reducing her reliance on finite water sources. She reused and repurposed items whenever possible, minimizing her contribution to the landfill.

But perhaps most importantly, Old Mother Wilderness shared her wisdom and knowledge with others, teaching them the importance of living in harmony with nature and respecting the earth that sustains us all. She welcomed visitors to her wilderness home, offering them guidance and insight into the ways of the natural world.

For Old Mother Wilderness, the wilderness was not just a place to live – it was a teacher, a guide, a source of wisdom and inspiration. And as she walked through the forest, surrounded by the sights and sounds of the natural world, she knew that she was exactly where she was meant to be – at home, in the heart of nature.

And though her days in the wilderness were numbered, she knew that her legacy would live on – in the trees she planted, in the animals she cared for, in the lessons she shared with others. For Old Mother Wilderness, the wilderness was not just a place to live – it was a way of life, a philosophy, a legacy that would endure for generations to come.

In the quiet moments of the evening, as the sun dipped below the horizon and the stars began to twinkle overhead, Old Mother Wilderness would sit by the fire, lost in thought. And as she closed her eyes and listened to the gentle sounds of the forest around her, she felt a sense of peace wash over her – a deep-rooted certainty that she was exactly where she was meant to be.

She would reflect on the day's events, on the beauty and wonder of the natural world, on the lessons she had learned and the connections she had made. She would give thanks for the blessings of the earth – for the sun that warmed her skin, for the rain that nourished the soil, for the wind that whispered through the trees.

And as she sat by the fire, surrounded by the sights, and sounds of the wilderness, Old Mother Wilderness felt a profound sense of gratitude wash over her – gratitude for the beauty and wonder of the world in which she lived, for the peace and tranquillity of the natural world, for the simple joys of life.

For in the heart of the wilderness, Old Mother Wilderness had found something truly precious – a sense of belonging, a sense of purpose, a sense of connection to the natural world that sustained her through even the darkest of days. And as she sat by the fire, surrounded by the sights and sounds of the forest, she knew that she was exactly where she was meant to be – at home, in the heart of nature.

And though her days in the wilderness were numbered, she knew that she would carry the lessons she had learned with her wherever she went. For Old Mother Wilderness had found a kind of peace and contentment in the natural world that she had never known before, a sense of harmony and balance that filled her with a deep sense of joy and fulfillment.

And as she closed her eyes and listened to the gentle sounds of the forest around her, Old Mother Wilderness felt a sense of gratitude wash over her – gratitude for the beauty and wonder of the natural world, for the peace and tranquility of the wilderness, for the simple joys of life. And in that moment, she knew that she was exactly where she was meant to be – at home, in the heart of nature.

For in the heart of the wilderness, amidst the towering trees and the gentle rustle of leaves, Old Mother Wilderness had found her home. And though her days may have been filled with solitude, they were also filled with purpose, meaning, and a profound sense of connection to the world around her.

In the quiet solitude of the forest, Old Mother Wilderness had discovered a sense of peace and contentment that she had never known before. She had learned to listen to the rhythms of nature, to pay attention to the subtle whispers of the wind and the soft murmur of the stream. And in doing so, she had found a sense of belonging that she had never thought possible.

She had come to understand that she was not separate from the natural world, but rather a part of it – a single thread woven into the vast tapestry of life. And though her days may have been filled with solitude, she was never truly alone, for she was surrounded by the sights and sounds of the wilderness, by the gentle embrace of the earth itself.

And as she walked through the forest, she felt a sense of kinship with every living thing she encountered – the trees that reached for the sky, the birds that sang in the branches, the animals that scurried through the underbrush. She knew that they were all connected, all part of the same intricate web of life that sustained the world around her.

In the heart of the wilderness, Old Mother Wilderness had found a sense of purpose and meaning that she had never known before. She had come to understand that her life was intertwined with the lives of all living things, that her actions had the power to shape the world around her in profound ways.

And though her days in the wilderness were numbered, she knew that her legacy would endure – in the trees she had planted, in the animals she had cared for, in the lessons she had shared with others. For Old Mother Wilderness had found her home in the heart of the wilderness, and there she would remain, forever a part of the natural world that had welcomed her with open arms.

As she looked out over the forest that stretched endlessly before her, Old Mother Wilderness felt a sense of gratitude wash over her – gratitude for the beauty of the world around her, for the peace and tranquility of the wilderness, for the rhythms of nature that sustained her through even the darkest of days.

She watched as the sunlight filtered through the trees, casting dappled patterns of light and shadow on the forest floor. She listened to the gentle rustle of leaves in the breeze, the distant call of a bird in the treetops, the soft gurgle of the stream as it wound its way through the landscape.

And in that moment, surrounded by the sights and sounds of the wilderness, Old Mother Wilderness felt a deep sense of connection to the world around her. She knew that she was but a small part of a much larger whole, a single thread woven into the intricate tapestry of life.

But she also knew that her presence in the wilderness mattered – that her actions had the power to shape the world around her in profound ways. And so, she lived her life with intention and purpose, striving to leave behind a legacy of harmony and balance, of respect and reverence for the natural world.

For Old Mother Wilderness, the wilderness was not just a place to live – it was a way of life, a philosophy, a way of being in the world. And as she stood on the edge of the forest, surrounded by the sights and sounds of the natural world, she knew that she was exactly where she was meant to be – at home, in the heart of nature.

And though her days in the wilderness were numbered, she knew that her legacy would live on – in the trees she had planted, in the animals she had cared for, in the lessons she had shared with others. For Old Mother Wilderness had found her home in the heart of the wilderness, and there she would remain, forever a part of the natural world that had welcomed her with open arms.

And as the fire crackled and the stars shone brightly overhead, Old Mother Wilderness closed her eyes and whispered a silent prayer of thanks to the universe. For she knew that in the heart of the wilderness, amidst the beauty and wonder of the natural world, she had found her true home – a place of peace, of belonging, and of endless possibility.

In that moment of quiet reflection, surrounded by the sights and sounds of the forest, Old Mother Wilderness felt a profound sense of gratitude wash over her. She was grateful for the beauty of the world around her, for the peace and tranquility of the wilderness, for the rhythms of nature that sustained her through even the darkest of days.

She was grateful for the lessons she had learned and the connections she had made, for the friendships she had forged and the memories she had created. And she was grateful for the sense of purpose and meaning that the wilderness had brought into her life, for the deep sense of belonging that she felt amidst the towering trees and meandering streams.

For Old Mother Wilderness, the wilderness was not just a place to live – it was a way of life, a philosophy, a legacy that would endure for generations to come. And as she sat by the fire, surrounded by the sights and sounds of the natural world, she knew that she was exactly where she was meant to be – at home, in the heart of nature.

And though her days in the wilderness were numbered, she knew that her legacy would live on – in the trees she had planted, in the animals she had cared for, in the lessons she had shared with others. For Old Mother Wilderness had found her true home in the heart of the wilderness, and there she would remain, forever a part of the natural world that had welcomed her with open arms.

And so, she sat in the quiet darkness, surrounded by the gentle embrace of the forest, and allowed herself to be carried away by the rhythms of nature. For in that moment, she was at one with the world around her, connected to every living thing by the invisible threads of life that bound them together in a tapestry of existence. And as she drifted off to sleep, cradled in the arms of the wilderness, she knew that she was exactly where she was meant to be – at home, in the heart of the natural world.

In the stillness of the night, Old Mother Wilderness felt a profound sense of peace settle over her. She listened to the soft rustle of leaves in the breeze, the distant hoot of an owl in the treetops, the steady rhythm of her own heartbeat. And as she closed her eyes and surrendered herself to the embrace of sleep, she felt a deep sense of contentment wash over her – a quiet assurance that she was exactly where she was meant to be.

For in the heart of the wilderness, amidst the beauty and wonder of the natural world, Old Mother Wilderness had found her true home. She had discovered a sense of belonging that she had never known before, a connection to the world around her that filled her with a profound sense of peace and contentment.

And as she drifted off to sleep, surrounded by the sights and sounds of the forest, she knew that she was exactly where she was meant to be – at one with the natural world, in perfect harmony with its rhythms and cycles. And though her days in the wilderness were numbered, she knew that she would carry the lessons she had learned with her wherever she went, for she had found her true home in the heart of the natural world.

# The Call of the Wild

Chapter 4:

In the heart of the wilderness, where the only sounds were those of nature's symphony, Old Mother Wilderness found herself tested by the raw forces of the natural world. Each day brought its own set of challenges, from sudden storms to unexpected encounters with wild animals. Yet, she faced these trials with a determination born of a lifetime spent in communion with the wild.

As the seasons changed and the weather grew harsh, Old Mother Wilderness felt the full brunt of nature's fury. She braved fierce winds that whipped through the trees, pelting her with icy rain and snow. She endured bitter cold that seeped into her bones, numbing her fingers and toes. And yet, amidst the harshness of winter, she found a quiet beauty in the snow-covered landscape, a serenity that could only be found in the heart of the wilderness.

Each day began with the same ritual – rising before dawn to tend to the chores that kept her alive. She hunted for her food, tracking deer through the dense underbrush or trapping rabbits in simple snares. She tended to her modest garden, coaxing vegetables from the rocky soil and harvesting herbs for seasoning. And she gathered firewood, chopping down trees and splitting logs with practiced efficiency, knowing that the warmth of the fire was her only defense against the biting cold of winter nights.

But it was not just the physical challenges that tested Old Mother Wilderness – it was the emotional toll of living alone in the vast expanse of the wilderness. She grappled with feelings of loneliness and isolation, longing for the companionship of her husband, who had been her constant companion for so many years. Yet, even in her darkest moments, she found solace in the embrace of nature, drawing strength from the silent majesty of the forest that surrounded her.

And so, day by day, Old Mother Wilderness faced the challenges of life in the wilderness with unwavering resilience. She weathered the storms that raged around her, both literal and metaphorical, drawing on the lessons of survival that she had learned over a lifetime spent in communion with the wild. And though the road ahead was fraught with uncertainty, she knew that she possessed the strength and courage to face whatever obstacles lay in her path, for she was a daughter of the wilderness, and the wilderness was her home.

As the seasons shifted and the landscape transformed, Old Mother Wilderness adapted to the ever-changing rhythm of life in the wilderness. In the spring, she reveled in the abundance of new growth, foraging for wild greens and tender shoots to supplement her diet. With each passing day, she watched as the forest came alive with the sights and sounds of new life, a testament to the resilience of nature in the face of adversity.

But as the days grew longer and the temperatures soared, Old Mother Wilderness knew that she must prepare for the challenges that lay ahead. She tended to her garden with care, planting crops that would sustain her through the long winter months. And as she worked the soil with her weathered hands, she felt a sense of connection to the land that sustained her, a deep appreciation for the beauty and bounty of the natural world.

Throughout the summer months, Old Mother Wilderness toiled under the hot sun, tending to her crops and gathering food for the months ahead. She spent long days in the fields, harvesting vegetables and fruits, and preserving them for the winter months. She knew that her survival depended on her ability to store enough food to last through the long, cold winters that blanketed the wilderness in a blanket of snow.

But despite the challenges of living off the land, Old Mother Wilderness found joy in the simple pleasures of life in the wilderness. She relished the taste of fresh-picked berries and the smell of wildflowers blooming in the meadows. She marveled at the sight of animals frolicking in the fields and birds soaring overhead. And as she worked, she sang songs of gratitude to the earth that sustained her, offering thanks for the abundance of nature that surrounded her.

As the summer faded into autumn, Old Mother Wilderness felt a sense of urgency settle over the land. She knew that winter was fast approaching, and that she must gather enough food and supplies to last through the long months of cold and darkness. She worked tirelessly, harvesting the last of her crops and gathering firewood to keep her warm through the winter nights. And as she watched the leaves change from green to gold, she felt a sense of peace settle over the land, a quiet acceptance of the changing seasons and the cycle of life and death that governed the wilderness.

And so, as the days grew shorter and the nights grew colder, Old Mother Wilderness prepared herself for the challenges that lay ahead. She knew that the winter would be long and harsh, but she also knew that she possessed the strength and resilience to endure whatever came her way. For she was a daughter of the wilderness, and the wilderness was her home.

As summer gave way to autumn, Old Mother Wilderness felt the first hints of change in the air. The days grew shorter, the nights grew colder, and the forest was painted in hues of red, orange, and gold. Yet, amidst the beauty of the changing seasons, there lingered a sense of urgency – a reminder that winter was fast approaching, and with it, the need to prepare for the challenges that lay ahead.

And so, Old Mother Wilderness set about gathering the resources she would need to weather the long, cold months ahead. She ventured deep into the forest, her keen eyes scanning the landscape for signs of edible plants and mushrooms. She gathered berries and nuts, storing them away in jars and baskets to supplement her meagre diet.

Each day, she rose before dawn and set out into the wilderness, her footsteps echoing through the silent woods. She climbed hills and crossed streams, following the ancient paths that crisscrossed the land. And with each step, she felt a sense of purpose and determination grow within her – for she knew that her survival depended on her ability to gather enough food to last through the winter.

As the days grew shorter and the nights grew colder, Old Mother Wilderness redoubled her efforts, pushing herself to the limits of her endurance. She climbed trees to reach the highest branches, searching for nuts and berries hidden among the leaves. She dug through the underbrush, her hands stained with the earth, searching for roots and tubers buried beneath the soil.

And as she worked, she sang songs of thanks to the earth that sustained her, offering gratitude for the bounty of nature that surrounded her. She felt a deep connection to the land, a sense of belonging that transcended words – for she knew that she was a part of something greater than herself, a part of the intricate web of life that bound all living things together.

As autumn gave way to winter, Old Mother Wilderness retreated to the safety of her cabin, her arms laden with the fruits of her labor. She stacked firewood by the hearth and filled her pantry with jars of preserved food, readying herself for the long, cold months that lay ahead. And as the first snowflakes began to fall outside, she felt a sense of peace settle over her – for she knew that she was prepared for whatever challenges winter might bring.

And so, as the world outside grew quiet and still, Old Mother Wilderness settled in for the winter, her heart filled with gratitude for the beauty and wonder of the natural world, and for the strength and resilience that had carried her through another season in the wilderness. For she was a daughter of the wilderness, and the wilderness was her home.

But it was not just food that Old Mother Wilderness needed to survive the harsh winter months – she also needed fuel to keep her warm through the cold, dark nights. And so, she set out to gather firewood, scouring the forest for fallen branches and deadwood that she could use to fuel her hearth.

With each log she added to her pile, Old Mother Wilderness felt a sense of satisfaction – a tangible reminder of her ability to provide for herself in the face of adversity. For in the heart of the wilderness, where every day was a struggle for survival, she had learned to rely on her own strength and ingenuity to overcome whatever challenges came her way.

She chopped and stacked wood with practiced efficiency, her muscles aching from the exertion but her spirits high. For she knew that the warmth of the fire would not only keep her physically comfortable but would also provide a sense of security and safety in the long, dark nights of winter.

As she worked, she thought back to the lessons her husband had taught her about surviving in the wilderness. He had been her mentor and her guide, showing her how to navigate the forests, track animals, and live off the land. And though he was no longer by her side, his teachings lived on in her, guiding her through each new challenge she faced.

With each armful of wood she gathered, Old Mother Wilderness felt a sense of connection to the land – a deep appreciation for the beauty and bounty of the natural world that sustained her. For in the heart of the wilderness, she had found not just a place to live, but a home – a sanctuary where she could truly be herself, free from the constraints of society and the burdens of the modern world.

And so, as she stacked the final log on her pile and watched the flames dance in the hearth, Old Mother Wilderness felt a sense of gratitude wash over her – gratitude for the simple pleasures of life in the wilderness, for the challenges that had made her strong, and for the beauty of the natural world that surrounded her. For she was a daughter of the wilderness, and the wilderness was her home.

As the days grew shorter and the nights grew colder, Old Mother Wilderness knew that she must make the most of the remaining daylight hours. She worked tirelessly from dawn until dusk, gathering food, tending to her garden, and stockpiling firewood for the long winter ahead.

And though the work was hard and the days were long, Old Mother Wilderness found solace in the knowledge that she was preparing herself for the challenges that lay ahead. For in the heart of the wilderness, where the only law was the law of nature, she knew that survival depended on her ability to adapt and thrive in even the harshest of conditions.

Each day brought its own set of tasks and challenges, from tending to her crops to repairing the roof of her cabin. And though the work was often physically demanding, Old Mother Wilderness faced it with a quiet determination, drawing on the strength and resilience that had carried her through so many trials before.

As she worked, she felt a sense of connection to the land – a deep appreciation for the beauty and bounty of the natural world that surrounded her. She marveled at the intricacies of nature, from the delicate beauty of a snowflake to the raw power of a thunderstorm. And with each passing day, she grew more in tune with the rhythms of the wilderness, learning to anticipate its moods and its whims.

But amidst the beauty of the wilderness, there were also dangers lurking in the shadows. Old Mother Wilderness knew that she must always be on guard, for the forest was home to predators both great and small. She kept a keen eye out for signs of danger, listening for the telltale rustle of leaves or the faint growl of a distant predator.

And though the nights were long and the days were hard, Old Mother Wilderness found comfort in the knowledge that she was not alone. She felt a sense of kinship with the creatures of the forest, from the smallest insects to the largest predators. And in their company, she found solace and companionship amidst the vast expanse of the wilderness.

And so, as the days grew shorter and the nights grew colder, Old Mother Wilderness worked tirelessly to prepare herself for the challenges that lay ahead. For in the heart of the wilderness, where the only law was the law of nature, she knew that survival depended on her ability to adapt and thrive in even the harshest of conditions.

As winter descended upon the wilderness, Old Mother Wilderness retreated to the warmth and safety of her cabin, where she would wait out the long, cold months until spring returned once more. She huddled by the fire, wrapped in blankets and furs, as the wind howled outside and the snow piled up against the walls of her cabin.

But even in the depths of winter, Old Mother Wilderness found moments of beauty and wonder amidst the harshness of the natural world. She marveled at the delicate patterns of frost on the windowpanes, the shimmering blanket of snow that covered the forest floor, the crisp, clean scent of the air.

In the quiet solitude of her cabin, Old Mother Wilderness found solace in the simple routines of daily life. She brewed pots of hot tea to warm her chilled bones and cooked hearty stews over the crackling fire. She read books by the light of the flickering flames, losing herself in tales of far-off lands and daring adventures.

But amidst the comfort of her cabin, there were also challenges to be faced. The harshness of winter brought with it the constant threat of cold and hunger, as Old Mother Wilderness struggled to keep her fire burning and her pantry stocked with food. She rationed her supplies carefully, making every scrap of food and fuel last as long as possible.

Yet, despite the hardships of winter, Old Mother Wilderness remained resilient in the face of adversity. She drew on the strength and resourcefulness that had carried her through so many trials before, refusing to be daunted by the challenges of the cold and the snow.

And as she waited patiently for the return of spring, Old Mother Wilderness found comfort in the knowledge that she was not alone. She knew that the wilderness was alive with the promise of new life, even in the darkest days of winter, and that soon the forest would burst forth once more with the vibrant colors and sweet scents of spring.

And though the days were short and the nights were long, Old Mother Wilderness found comfort in the simple rhythms of life in the wilderness. She tended to her fire, cooked simple meals over the flames, and spent long hours lost in thought, reflecting on the beauty and wonder of the natural world.

For in the heart of the wilderness, where the only sounds were those of the wind in the trees and the crackling of the fire, Old Mother Wilderness found a sense of peace and contentment that she had never known before. And as she sat by the fire, surrounded by the sights and sounds of the wilderness, she knew that she was exactly where she was meant to be – at home, in the heart of nature.

In those quiet moments by the fire, Old Mother Wilderness felt a deep connection to the land and all the creatures that called it home. She listened to the howl of the wind outside and the creaking of the trees, feeling a sense of kinship with the ancient rhythms of the forest.

As she watched the flames dance and flicker in the hearth, Old Mother Wilderness found herself lost in thought, her mind wandering through the memories of seasons past. She thought of the summers spent basking in the warmth of the sun, the autumns filled with the vibrant colors of falling leaves, and the winters shrouded in a blanket of snow.

And though she missed the beauty of spring and the promise of new life, Old Mother Wilderness knew that each season had its own unique beauty and purpose. She embraced the stillness of winter, finding solace in the quiet solitude of the wilderness.

And as she sat by the fire, wrapped in blankets and furs, Old Mother Wilderness felt a sense of gratitude wash over her – gratitude for the simple pleasures of life in the wilderness, for the challenges that had made her strong, and for the beauty of the natural world that surrounded her. For she was a daughter of the wilderness, and the wilderness was her home.

But even in the tranquility of her cabin, Old Mother Wilderness could not escape the call of the wild – the primal urge that stirred within her, driving her to venture forth into the wilderness once more. And so, as soon as the snow began to melt and the days grew longer, she emerged from her cabin, ready to face whatever challenges the natural world had in store.

With each passing day, as the grip of winter loosened its hold on the land, Old Mother Wilderness felt a renewed sense of vitality coursing through her veins. She welcomed the warmth of the sun on her face and the fresh scent of spring in the air, eager to immerse herself once again in the beauty and wonder of the wilderness.

As she ventured deeper into the forest, Old Mother Wilderness marveled at the signs of new life emerging all around her. Tender green shoots pushed their way through the thawing earth, while buds blossomed on the branches of trees, casting a delicate hue of pink and white against the blue sky.

The forest echoed with the songs of birds returning from their winter migrations, their melodic calls filling the air with a symphony of sound. And as Old Mother Wilderness listened to their sweet melodies, she felt a sense of joy and renewal wash over her – a reminder that life, like the seasons, was ever-changing and full of possibility.

With each step she took, Old Mother Wilderness felt a sense of freedom and exhilaration, as though she were shedding the weight of winter and embracing the boundless potential of spring. And as she walked, she knew that she was not alone – for the wilderness was alive with the promise of new beginnings, and she was ready to embrace whatever adventures lay ahead.

With the arrival of spring, Old Mother Wilderness emerged from her cabin, ready to once again embrace the wilds that surrounded her. The forest, once cloaked in a blanket of snow, now burst forth with new life, the air filled with the sweet scent of blossoms and the joyful chirping of birds.

Old Mother Wilderness wasted no time in resuming her daily routines, venturing out into the forest to gather wild herbs and mushrooms, and tending to her garden with care. Each day brought new discoveries as the forest awoke from its winter slumber, and Old Mother Wilderness reveled in the beauty and abundance of the natural world.

With each passing day, the forest transformed before her eyes, as trees unfurled their leaves and flowers bloomed in riotous colors. Old Mother Wilderness marveled at the vibrant hues of the wildflowers that carpeted the forest floor, their delicate petals nodding in the breeze.

But amidst the beauty of spring, there were also challenges to be faced. Old Mother Wilderness knew that she must remain vigilant against the dangers that lurked in the wilderness, from sudden storms to encounters with wild animals. She kept a keen eye out for signs of danger, listening for the telltale rustle of leaves or the distant call of a predator.

Yet, despite the risks, Old Mother Wilderness felt a sense of exhilaration as she explored the forest once more. She drank in the sights and sounds of spring, feeling a deep connection to the land and all the creatures that called it home.

And as she walked, she knew that she was exactly where she was meant to be – at home, in the heart of the wilderness, surrounded by the beauty and wonder of the natural world.

But amidst the beauty of spring, there lingered a sense of urgency – a reminder that time was fleeting, and that she must make the most of the fleeting moments before summer's heat descended upon the land. And so, Old Mother Wilderness set about preparing for the challenges that lay ahead, gathering food and firewood, and tending to her garden with care.

With each passing day, the sun climbed higher in the sky, casting its warm rays down upon the forest below. Old Mother Wilderness felt the earth come alive beneath her feet, as the plants in her garden responded eagerly to the nourishing touch of the sun.

She worked tirelessly, planting seeds and pulling weeds, coaxing the earth to yield its bounty once more. She knew that her survival depended on the fruits of her labor, and she was determined to do whatever it took to ensure that her pantry was stocked with food for the long months ahead.

And as she worked, Old Mother Wilderness felt a sense of satisfaction wash over her – a deep-rooted certainty that she was doing exactly what she was meant to be doing. For in the heart of the wilderness, where every day was a struggle for survival, she had learned to trust in the rhythms of nature and the wisdom of her own instincts.

And so, she worked tirelessly, driven by a sense of purpose and a deep love for the land that sustained her. And as the days grew longer and the nights grew shorter, Old Mother Wilderness knew that she was ready to face whatever challenges the wilderness had in store. For she was a daughter of the wilderness, and the wilderness was her home.

As the days grew longer and the temperatures soared, Old Mother Wilderness felt a sense of anticipation building within her – a longing to once again heed the call of the wild and venture forth into the untamed wilderness. And so, as soon as the last frost had melted and the ground had thawed, she set out into the forest, eager to explore the world that lay beyond her cabin door.

With each step she took, Old Mother Wilderness felt a sense of freedom and exhilaration wash over her – a reminder that she was a creature of the wild, born to roam the untamed landscapes of the natural world. And though the journey ahead would be long and difficult, she knew that she was ready to face whatever challenges came her way, for she was a daughter of the wilderness, and the wilderness was her home.

The forest welcomed her with open arms, its ancient trees towering above her like sentinels of the wild. The air was alive with the songs of birds and the chatter of small animals, and the earth beneath her feet pulsed with the rhythm of life. Old Mother Wilderness drank in the sights and sounds of the forest, feeling a deep sense of connection to the land and all the creatures that called it home.

As she walked, she felt the weight of the world lift from her shoulders, replaced by a sense of peace and tranquility that she could only find in the heart of the wilderness. She let the wind guide her, following the meandering paths of the forest as they wound their way through the ancient trees and overgrown underbrush.

And as she walked, Old Mother Wilderness felt a sense of purpose settle over her – a knowing that she was exactly where she was meant to be, doing exactly what she was meant to do. For in the heart of the wilderness, where every step was a journey and every breath was a blessing, she had found her true home.

As she ventured deeper into the forest, Old Mother Wilderness felt a sense of wonder and awe wash over her – a reminder of the vastness and beauty of the natural world. She marveled at the towering trees that stretched towards the sky, their branches reaching out like the arms of an old friend. She listened to the gentle rustle of leaves in the breeze, the distant call of a bird in the treetops, the soft gurgle of a nearby stream.

With each passing moment, Old Mother Wilderness felt more alive than she had in years, as though the very essence of the wilderness flowed through her veins. And though the journey ahead would be long and difficult, she knew that she was exactly where she was meant to be – at home, in the heart of nature.

The forest embraced her with its sights and sounds, offering a sense of peace and tranquility that she could find nowhere else. She followed the winding paths of the forest, letting her instincts guide her as she explored the untamed landscapes that stretched out before her.

And as she walked, Old Mother Wilderness felt a sense of kinship with the creatures that called the forest home. She watched as deer bounded through the underbrush, their graceful movements a testament to the beauty of the natural world. She listened as birds sang their sweet melodies, their songs echoing through the trees like whispers of the wind.

In the heart of the wilderness, where the only sounds were those of nature's symphony, Old Mother Wilderness felt a sense of belonging that she had never known before. For in the heart of nature, surrounded by the beauty and wonder of the wild, she had found her true home.

But as Old Mother Wilderness ventured deeper into the forest, she soon realized that the wilderness held many secrets – some beautiful, and some dangerous. She encountered wild animals in their natural habitat, from deer and rabbits to bears and wolves, each one a testament to the untamed beauty of the natural world.

Yet, amidst the dangers of the wilderness, there also lay moments of unexpected beauty and wonder. Old Mother Wilderness stumbled upon hidden waterfalls cascading down moss-covered cliffs, and stumbled upon hidden glades filled with wildflowers and butterflies. And though the journey ahead would be fraught with challenges, she knew that she was ready to face whatever obstacles came her way, for she was a daughter of the wilderness, and the wilderness was her home.

With each step she took, Old Mother Wilderness felt a sense of exhilaration coursing through her veins – a reminder that she was alive, truly alive, in a way that she had never felt before. She drank in the sights and sounds of the forest, letting them wash over her like a healing balm, soothing her weary soul and filling her with a sense of renewed purpose.

And though the journey ahead would be long and difficult, she knew that she was not alone. For in the heart of the wilderness, where every tree and every rock seemed to pulse with life, she felt a sense of connection to the world around her – a sense of belonging that she had never known before.

And so, with a heart full of hope and a spirit filled with determination, Old Mother Wilderness pressed on, ready to face whatever challenges lay ahead. For she knew that in the heart of the wilderness, where the only law was the law of nature, she would always find her true home.

As she journeyed deeper into the heart of the forest, Old Mother Wilderness found herself drawn to the ancient groves that lay hidden deep within its depths. Here, the trees towered overhead, their branches reaching towards the sky like the fingers of giants. Moss-covered rocks jutted out from the forest floor, and the air was thick with the scent of earth and pine.

In the heart of these ancient groves, Old Mother Wilderness felt a sense of reverence wash over her – a reminder of the timeless beauty and majesty of the natural world. She wandered through the forest, her senses alive to the sights and sounds around her, as though she were walking through a dream.

The trees whispered secrets to her as she passed, their leaves rustling in the breeze like the s of an ancient tome. She paused to run her fingers over the rough bark of an old oak, feeling the pulse of life beneath her touch. She listened to the songs of the birds, their melodies weaving through the air like threads of gold.

And as she walked, Old Mother Wilderness felt a sense of peace settle over her – a deep-rooted calm that she could only find in the heart of the wilderness. Here, amidst the ancient groves, she felt a connection to something greater than herself – a sense of belonging that transcended time and space.

In the heart of the forest, where the only sounds were those of nature's symphony, Old Mother Wilderness felt a sense of wonder and awe wash over her. For in that moment, she knew that she was exactly where she was meant to be – at home, in the heart of the natural world.

And as she wandered deeper into the heart of the forest, Old Mother Wilderness felt a sense of peace settle over her – a quiet assurance that she was exactly where she was meant to be. For in the heart of the wilderness, where every step brought her closer to the natural world, she felt a deep sense of belonging that she had never known before.

The forest welcomed her with open arms, embracing her in its gentle embrace and whispering secrets that only those who listened with an open heart could hear. She felt the rhythm of the earth beneath her feet, the pulse of life that flowed through every living thing around her.

As she walked, Old Mother Wilderness found herself lost in the beauty of the forest – the dappled sunlight filtering through the canopy above, the scent of pine needles and wildflowers mingling in the air, the gentle rustle of leaves as the wind danced through the trees.

And as she moved through the forest, Old Mother Wilderness felt her worries and cares fall away, replaced by a sense of peace and tranquility that she could find nowhere else. Here, amidst the ancient trees and hidden glades, she was free to be herself – to revel in the beauty of the natural world and to embrace the wildness that lay within her soul.

For in the heart of the wilderness, where the only sounds were those of nature's symphony, Old Mother Wilderness found a sense of peace and contentment that she had never known before. And as she walked, she knew that she was exactly where she was meant to be – at home, in the heart of the forest, surrounded by the beauty and wonder of the natural world.

With each step she took, Old Mother Wilderness felt a deepening connection to the wilderness surrounding her. The rustle of leaves beneath her feet, the whisper of the wind through the branches, and the distant call of birds in the canopy above all spoke to her in a language as old as time itself. She moved through the forest with a sense of purpose, guided by an intuition honed through years of living in harmony with the natural world.

As she walked, memories of past journeys through the wilderness flooded her mind. She recalled the feeling of freedom that came with each step, the exhilaration of exploring uncharted territory, and the sense of wonder that filled her heart at every new discovery. Each journey had been a testament to her resilience and resourcefulness, a reaffirmation of her deep connection to the wild.

She remembered the time she had tracked a deer through the dense underbrush, her senses alive to the subtle clues left behind by the creature's passing. She remembered the thrill of the chase, the rush of adrenaline as she closed in on her quarry, and the satisfaction of finally bringing home a prize to sustain her through the long winter months.

She remembered the countless nights spent under the stars, the crackling of the campfire the only sound in the silent wilderness. She remembered the feeling of peace that washed over her as she lay beneath the vast expanse of the night sky, the stars twinkling overhead like diamonds scattered across a velvet blanket.

And she remembered the countless times she had lost herself in the beauty of the natural world, the sense of awe and wonder that filled her soul as she beheld the majesty of the mountains, the grandeur of the forests, and the power of the rivers that carved their way through the landscape.

As she walked, Old Mother Wilderness felt the weight of these memories settle upon her like a familiar cloak, comforting and reassuring in their familiarity. And though each journey had been unique, they all shared one common thread – the call of the wild, beckoning her ever onward, ever deeper into the heart of the wilderness.

But as Old Mother Wilderness journeyed deeper into the heart of the forest, she also encountered challenges that tested her strength and resolve. She traversed rugged terrain, crossed rushing rivers, and navigated dense undergrowth, all while keeping a watchful eye out for signs of danger. Yet, despite the obstacles that lay in her path, she pressed onward, driven by a determination to explore the wilderness to its fullest extent.

Along the way, she encountered a myriad of creatures, each one a testament to the diversity and resilience of life in the forest. She observed the graceful movements of deer as they bounded through the underbrush, the playful antics of squirrels as they leapt from branch to branch, and the majestic flight of birds as they soared overhead. Each encounter served as a reminder of the interconnectedness of all living things, and the delicate balance that sustained life in the wilderness.

As she journeyed deeper into the heart of the forest, Old Mother Wilderness found herself faced with new challenges at every turn. She encountered treacherous cliffs and steep inclines, dense thickets of brambles and thorns, and swift-flowing rivers that threatened to sweep her away in their powerful currents. Yet, with each obstacle she overcame, she grew stronger and more determined, her resolve unshaken by the trials of the wilderness.

Despite the hardships she faced, Old Mother Wilderness found solace in the beauty and majesty of the natural world that surrounded her. She marveled at the towering trees that reached towards the sky, their branches intertwining to form a canopy overhead. She listened to the gentle rustle of leaves in the breeze, the soft murmur of water as it cascaded over rocks in a nearby stream, and the distant call of birdsong echoing through the forest.

With each step she took, Old Mother Wilderness felt herself drawn deeper into the heart of the wilderness, her senses alive to the sights, sounds, and smells of the natural world. She breathed in the earthy scent of moss and pine, felt the cool touch of the forest floor beneath her feet, and listened to the symphony of life that surrounded her. And though the journey ahead was long and difficult, she knew that she was exactly where she was meant to be – at home, in the heart of nature.

Old Mother Wilderness felt a profound sense of awe wash over her. She marveled at the towering trees that surrounded her, their branches reaching towards the sky like the spires of a cathedral. She listened to the symphony of sounds that filled the air – the gentle rustle of leaves, the melodic chirping of birds, the distant rush of water.

With each passing moment, she felt more alive than she had in years, as though the very essence of the wilderness flowed through her veins. And though the journey ahead would be long and arduous, she knew that she was exactly where she was meant to be – at home, in the heart of nature.

As she continued her journey through the forest, Old Mother Wilderness found herself drawn deeper into its embrace. She followed winding trails that led through ancient groves and hidden glades, her senses alive to the sights, sounds, and smells of the natural world around her. She paused often to take in her surroundings, to breathe in the earthy scent of moss and pine, to listen to the symphony of life that filled the air.

With each step she took, she felt a sense of peace settle over her – a quiet assurance that she was exactly where she was meant to be. For in the heart of the wilderness, where every moment was a testament to the beauty and majesty of the natural world, she felt a deep sense of belonging that she had never known before. And as she walked, guided by the rhythms of nature, she knew that she was on a journey that would forever change her, body and soul.

Old Mother Wilderness felt a sense of peace settle over her. She embraced the solitude of the wilderness, finding solace in the quiet beauty that surrounded her. She reveled in the simple pleasures of life in the wild – the warmth of the sun on her skin, the cool touch of the breeze, the earthy scent of the forest floor.

With each passing day, she felt more attuned to the rhythms of the natural world, more connected to the ancient forces that shaped the land. And though the journey ahead was uncertain, she knew that she was ready to face whatever challenges came her way, for she was a daughter of the wilderness, and the wilderness was her home.

As she journeyed deeper into the heart of the forest, Old Mother Wilderness encountered new wonders at every turn. She stumbled upon hidden streams that sparkled in the sunlight, and stumbled upon secret glens where wildflowers bloomed in riotous colors. She marveled at the intricate patterns of ferns that carpeted the forest floor, and listened to the symphony of sounds that filled the air – the chatter of squirrels, the trill of birds, the soft gurgle of water.

With each new discovery, she felt a sense of wonder and awe wash over her – a reminder of the beauty and diversity of life in the wilderness. And though the journey ahead was long and challenging, she knew that she was exactly where she was meant to be – at home, in the heart of nature.

Old Mother Wilderness felt a sense of reverence wash over her. She walked with a quiet humility, mindful of the sacredness of the land she traversed. She offered prayers of gratitude to the spirits of the forest, honoring the plants and animals that sustained her on her journey.

With each step she took, she felt a deeper connection to the natural world around her. She recognized herself not as an outsider, but as an integral part of the intricate web of life that spanned the forest. And though the journey ahead was filled with uncertainty, she knew that she was never truly alone, for she was surrounded by the spirits of the wilderness, guiding her every step of the way.

As she journeyed deeper into the heart of the forest, Old Mother Wilderness felt a sense of peace settle over her. She embraced the solitude of the wilderness, finding solace in the quiet beauty that surrounded her. She reveled in the simple pleasures of life in the wild – the warmth of the sun on her skin, the cool touch of the breeze, the earthy scent of the forest floor.

With each step she took, Old Mother Wilderness marveled at the beauty and complexity of the natural world. She gazed in awe at the towering mountains that loomed overhead, their snow-capped peaks reaching towards the sky. She listened to the soothing sound of cascading waterfalls, their rushing waters a symphony of nature's power and grace. And she admired the lush valleys that stretched out before her, their vibrant colors painting a picture of life and abundance.

In the presence of such majestic landscapes, Old Mother Wilderness felt a profound sense of humility. She realized how small she was in comparison to the vastness of the wilderness, how insignificant her worries and fears seemed in the grand scheme of things. And yet, she also felt a deep connection to the land, a sense of belonging that filled her heart with joy and gratitude.

As she continued on her journey, Old Mother Wilderness vowed to cherish every moment she spent in the wilderness, to savor the sights and sounds of nature's splendor. For in the heart of the wilderness, she knew that she was truly alive, truly free, and truly at home.

Old Mother Wilderness observed the playful antics of squirrels as they chased each other through the trees, their nimble movements a testament to their agility and grace. She watched with delight as the creatures leaped from branch to branch, their fluffy tails trailing behind them like banners of joy.

She marveled at the graceful movements of deer as they moved through the forest, their elegant strides a reminder of the beauty and majesty of the natural world. She admired the way they navigated the terrain with ease, their keen senses attuned to the slightest sound or movement.

And she was captivated by the majestic flight of birds as they soared overhead, their wings outstretched against the vast expanse of sky. She watched in awe as they circled and swooped, their calls echoing through the air like music from another world.

In the presence of these creatures, Old Mother Wilderness felt a deep sense of gratitude for the beauty and wonder of the natural world. She realized that each one was a part of the intricate tapestry of life that spanned the forest, each one playing a vital role in the delicate balance of nature. And as she continued on her journey, she vowed to cherish and protect the creatures that called the wilderness home, for they were as much a part of her world as she was theirs.

With each obstacle she faced, Old Mother Wilderness drew upon the lessons she had learned from a lifetime spent in communion with the wild. She trusted her intuition to lead her down the safest paths, her keen senses alert to the slightest changes in the environment around her.

She relied on her resourcefulness to overcome whatever challenges came her way, using her ingenuity to fashion tools and shelters from the materials she found in the forest. And she called upon her inner strength to persevere in the face of adversity, drawing courage from the knowledge that she was capable of overcoming any obstacle that stood in her path.

In these moments of serendipity, Old Mother Wilderness felt a deep sense of connection to the land and its inhabitants. She marveled at the intricate patterns of life that flourished in even the most remote corners of the forest, each one a testament to the resilience and adaptability of nature.

As she explored further, Old Mother Wilderness encountered signs of the forest's rich history – ancient trees bearing the scars of countless seasons, weathered rock formations etched with the passage of time, and remnants of long-forgotten civilizations hidden amidst the undergrowth. Each discovery spoke to her in a language as old as the earth itself, whispering tales of the land's storied past and the countless generations who had walked its paths before her.

With each new discovery, Old Mother Wilderness felt her connection to the natural world deepening. She saw herself not as a solitary traveler, but as part of a timeless tapestry of life that stretched back through the ages. And as she walked through the forest, she carried with her the knowledge that she was but one small part of a vast and wondrous universe, forever bound to the land that had nurtured her from birth.

With each passing day, Old Mother Wilderness felt herself becoming more attuned to the rhythms of the natural world. She learned to read the signs in the sky, the patterns in the wind, and the subtle shifts in the behavior of the animals around her. She discovered the art of survival in the wilderness, finding sustenance in the plants and animals that called the forest home.

But amidst the solitude, there were also moments of reflection and introspection. Old Mother Wilderness pondered the mysteries of life and death, the cycles of birth and rebirth that played out in the natural world around her. She found comfort in the knowledge that, like the trees that shed their leaves in autumn only to bloom again in spring, life was a constant cycle of endings and beginnings, of loss and renewal.

Old Mother Wilderness walked with reverence, her footsteps gentle upon the earth as she moved through the ancient groves and hidden glens of the forest. She felt the presence of the spirits all around her, in the rustle of leaves, the whisper of the wind, and the gentle murmur of the streams. With each passing moment, she felt more deeply connected to the natural world, more aware of the delicate balance that sustained life in the wilderness.

She paused often to offer prayers of gratitude to the spirits of the forest, honoring the plants and animals that sustained her on her journey. She thanked the trees for their shade and shelter, the animals for their companionship and wisdom, and the earth for its bounty and abundance. And as she spoke, she felt a sense of peace settle over her, a quiet assurance that she was exactly where she was meant to be.

With each step she took, she felt the bond between herself and the natural world grow stronger. She recognized herself not as an outsider, but as an integral part of the intricate web of life that spanned the forest. And though the journey ahead was filled with uncertainty, she knew that she was never truly alone, for she was surrounded by the spirits of the wilderness, guiding her every step of the way.

As she journeyed deeper into the wilderness, Old Mother Wilderness marveled at the grandeur of the natural world unfolding before her. Towering mountains loomed in the distance, their peaks reaching towards the sky like ancient sentinels guarding the secrets of the land. Cascading waterfalls tumbled down rocky cliffs, their crystalline waters shimmering in the sunlight as they flowed into meandering streams below. Lush valleys stretched out as far as the eye could see, carpeted with verdant forests and dotted with vibrant wildflowers.

With each passing moment, she felt more alive than she had in years, as though the very essence of the wilderness flowed through her veins. The beauty and complexity of the natural world filled her with a sense of wonder and awe, reminding her of the delicate balance that sustained life in the wilderness. She reveled in the symphony of sights and sounds around her, from the majestic peaks to the gentle rustle of leaves in the breeze.

And though the journey ahead was filled with challenges and obstacles, she knew that she was exactly where she was meant to be – at home, in the heart of nature. For in the wilderness, she found not only beauty and tranquility, but also a deep sense of purpose and belonging. And as she continued her journey, guided by the rhythms of the natural world, she embraced each new experience with open arms, eager to explore the wonders that awaited her in the wild.

With each step deeper into the wilderness, Old Mother Wilderness observed the intricate dance of life unfolding around her. Squirrels darted through the branches with nimble agility, their playful chattering echoing through the forest. Deer moved gracefully through the underbrush, their elegant strides carrying them effortlessly across the forest floor. Birds of all shapes and sizes filled the sky, their wings outstretched as they soared on unseen currents of air.

Each creature she encountered was a testament to the resilience and adaptability of life in the wilderness. From the smallest insect to the largest mammal, each played a vital role in the delicate balance of the ecosystem. Old Mother Wilderness watched with reverence as they went about their daily routines, marveling at the interconnectedness of all living things.

With each step, Old Mother Wilderness drew upon the lessons learned from a lifetime spent in communion with the natural world. She navigated the rugged terrain with the sure-footedness of one intimately familiar with the landscape, her movements guided by a deep-seated intuition honed through years of experience.

Crossing rushing rivers, she gauged the strength of the current with a practiced eye, choosing her path carefully to ensure safe passage. When sudden storms swept through the forest, she sought shelter beneath the canopy of towering trees, weathering the fury of the elements with stoic resolve.

Yet amidst the challenges, she found moments of unexpected beauty and wonder. She stumbled upon hidden glades carpeted with wildflowers, their vibrant colors a stark contrast to the verdant green of the surrounding forest. She marveled at the crystalline clarity of mountain streams, their waters teeming with life and vitality.

Each obstacle she encountered served as a reminder of the resilience and adaptability of life in the wilderness. And though the journey ahead was fraught with uncertainty, Old Mother Wilderness pressed onward, drawing strength from the land itself and the ancient wisdom it held.

As Old Mother Wilderness ventured deeper into the heart of the forest, each new discovery fueled her sense of wonder and reverence for the wilderness. In the hidden glades carpeted with wildflowers, she found herself surrounded by a riot of colors and scents, the air alive with the hum of bees and the fluttering of butterflies. Here, amidst the delicate blooms, she paused to marvel at the intricate patterns of petals and leaves, each one a masterpiece of nature's design.

Nearby, she stumbled upon hidden springs bubbling up from the earth, their waters crystal clear and cool to the touch. She cupped her hands and drank deeply, savoring the purity of the water and the rejuvenating energy it imparted. In these tranquil oases, she found respite from the rigors of her journey, the soothing sound of flowing water a balm for her weary soul.

In the depths of the forest, Old Mother Wilderness also encountered hidden caves filled with ancient rock formations, their walls adorned with stalactites and stalagmites formed over millennia. As she explored the shadowy depths, she felt a sense of awe and wonder wash over her, humbled by the sheer magnitude of time and the forces of nature that had shaped these subterranean wonders.

Each discovery served as a poignant reminder of the interconnectedness of all living things and the profound beauty that could be found in even the most unexpected places. And though the journey ahead was fraught with challenges and uncertainty, Old Mother Wilderness felt a renewed sense of purpose and determination as she continued to explore the untamed wilderness that lay before her.

With each passing day, Old Mother Wilderness embraced the solitude of the wilderness more deeply, finding solace in the quiet beauty that surrounded her. She reveled in the simple pleasures that life in the wild offered, finding contentment in the smallest of details. The warmth of the sun on her skin felt like a gentle caress, comforting her in moments of solitude and providing a sense of warmth and vitality.

The cool touch of the breeze whispered secrets of the forest, carrying with it the scents of pine and earth that filled her senses with a deep sense of peace. As she walked through the woods, she let the gentle rustle of leaves and the distant calls of birds lull her into a state of tranquility, grounding her in the present moment and reminding her of the beauty that surrounded her.

And as she lay beneath the canopy of trees, listening to the symphony of nature that played all around her, she felt a profound sense of gratitude well up within her. Gratitude for the simple pleasures of life – for the sun, the breeze, the earth – and for the opportunity to experience them in such abundance in the heart of the wilderness.

With each step she took, Old Mother Wilderness felt a sense of reverence for the land and its inhabitants deepen within her. She walked with a quiet humility, mindful of the sacredness of the natural world that surrounded her. Her heart overflowed with gratitude for the abundance of life that sustained her on her journey through the wilderness.

In moments of stillness, she offered prayers to the spirits of the forest, expressing her gratitude for the plants and animals that provided her with food, shelter, and companionship. She honored the ancient wisdom of the land, recognizing herself as just one small part of a vast and intricate ecosystem that thrived in harmony with the rhythms of nature.

With each prayer whispered into the wind, Old Mother Wilderness felt a deeper connection to the natural world around her. She felt the presence of the spirits of the forest guiding her every step, filling her with a sense of peace and purpose as she ventured deeper into the heart of the wilderness. And though the journey ahead was filled with challenges and uncertainties, she knew that she was never truly alone, for she was surrounded by the spirits of the wilderness, watching over her and guiding her on her journey.

As she continued her journey deeper into the forest, Old Mother Wilderness found herself surrounded by the awe-inspiring beauty of the natural world. Towering mountains loomed in the distance, their peaks crowned with snow, while cascading waterfalls sparkled like diamonds in the sunlight. Lush valleys stretched out before her, carpeted with verdant foliage and dotted with colorful wildflowers.

With each step she took, Old Mother Wilderness felt a profound sense of connection to the land around her. She marveled at the intricate web of life that sustained the wilderness, from the smallest insects to the largest predators. Every rock, every tree, every blade of grass seemed to pulse with the vibrant energy of the earth, filling her with a sense of wonder and reverence.

In the heart of the forest, where the only sounds were those of nature's symphony, Old Mother Wilderness felt truly alive. She drank in the sights and sounds of the wilderness with all her senses, allowing herself to be swept away by the beauty and majesty of the natural world. And though the journey ahead was filled with challenges and obstacles, she knew that she was exactly where she was meant to be – at home, in the heart of nature.

As she observed the playful antics of the forest creatures, Old Mother Wilderness couldn't help but smile. She felt a sense of kinship with the animals, recognizing their wild and free spirits as reflections of her own. The squirrels darted among the branches with nimble agility, their bushy tails twitching in excitement. The deer moved with grace and elegance, their eyes alert and their ears flicking at every sound.

And the birds danced through the sky with effortless grace, their wings slicing through the air like blades.

Each creature she encountered seemed to possess a unique personality, a testament to the diversity of life in the wilderness. Some were shy and elusive, darting away at the first sign of danger, while others were bold and curious, unafraid to approach and investigate this stranger in their midst. Yet, despite their differences, they all shared a common bond – a deep connection to the land that sustained them, and a fierce determination to survive and thrive in the face of adversity.

As Old Mother Wilderness watched the animals go about their daily routines, she felt a sense of gratitude wash over her. She was grateful for the opportunity to witness their beauty and grace, to share in their world for just a fleeting moment. And though the journey ahead was long and uncertain, she knew that she would carry these memories with her always, a reminder of the precious gift of life in the wilderness.

As she walked through the forest, Old Mother Wilderness felt a profound sense of reverence for the land and its inhabitants. She recognized herself as just one small part of a vast and intricate ecosystem, a single thread woven into the rich tapestry of life that stretched out before her. Each tree, each rock, each animal was a vital piece of the puzzle, contributing to the delicate balance that sustained the forest.

She walked with a quiet humility, mindful of the sacredness of the land she traversed. Every step she took was a tribute to the generations that had come before her, to the countless beings that had called this forest home long before she ever set foot in it. She offered prayers of gratitude to the spirits of the forest, honoring the plants and animals that sustained her on her journey.

With each passing moment, she felt a deeper connection to the natural world around her. She recognized herself not as an outsider, but as an integral part of the intricate web of life that spanned the forest.

And though the journey ahead was filled with uncertainty, she knew that she was never truly alone, for she was surrounded by the spirits of the wilderness, guiding her every step of the way.

These hidden treasures of the forest revealed themselves to Old Mother Wilderness like gifts from the earth itself, each one a testament to the mysteries that lay hidden just beyond the beaten path. In the hidden glades, she found herself surrounded by a riot of color as wildflowers stretched towards the sun, their petals unfurling in delicate shades of pink, purple, and yellow. The air was alive with the hum of bees and the flutter of butterflies, as though the forest itself was singing with joy.

Near the hidden springs, Old Mother Wilderness paused to drink from the crystal-clear waters that bubbled up from the earth, refreshing her body and soul with each cool sip. She marveled at the purity and clarity of the water, a reminder of the life-giving force that flowed through the heart of the wilderness. And as she drank, she felt a deep sense of gratitude welling up within her, a recognition of the interconnectedness of all living things.

In the hidden caves, she discovered ancient rock formations that spoke of the earth's long and storied history. Stalactites hung from the ceiling like icicles, while stalagmites rose from the floor like sentinels guarding the secrets of the underworld. The air was cool and still, and the only sound was the echo of her footsteps as she moved deeper into the darkness.

Each discovery filled Old Mother Wilderness with a sense of wonder and awe, a reminder of the boundless beauty and diversity of the natural world. And as she journeyed deeper into the heart of the forest, she carried these memories with her, treasures to cherish in the days and weeks to come.

As Old Mother Wilderness continued her journey through the wilderness, she found herself drawn deeper into the embrace of solitude. With each step she took, the cares of the world fell away, replaced by a profound sense of peace and tranquility. She reveled in the simple joys of life in the wild, finding solace in the gentle caress of the sun's rays, the cool touch of the breeze on her skin, and the earthy scent of the forest floor beneath her feet.

In these quiet moments, she felt a deep connection to the natural world around her, as though she were part of a grand symphony of life that played out in the wilderness. She listened to the rustle of leaves in the breeze, the distant call of birds in the canopy above, and the gentle murmur of a nearby stream. Each sound seemed to carry with it a message from the earth itself, a reminder of the interconnectedness of all living things.

With each step, Old Mother Wilderness offered silent prayers of gratitude to the spirits of the forest, honoring the land and its inhabitants for their generosity and sustenance. She understood the interconnectedness of all living things and felt a deep reverence for the natural world that surrounded her.

As she walked, she tread lightly upon the earth, mindful of her impact on the delicate ecosystems she traversed. She took only what she needed and left no trace of her passing, ensuring that the wilderness remained unspoiled for future generations to enjoy.

In this way, she lived in harmony with the land, embracing its rhythms and respecting its boundaries. She knew that she was but a small part of a vast and intricate web of life, and she walked with a sense of humility and gratitude for the opportunity to be a steward of the wilderness.

And though the path ahead was uncertain, Old Mother Wilderness walked with confidence, guided by the wisdom of the forest and the knowledge that she was never truly alone in her journey. For she walked in the company of the spirits of the wilderness, who whispered their secrets to her with every rustle of the leaves and every song of the birds.

EACH VISTA OLD MOTHER Wilderness encountered filled her with awe and wonder, reminding her of the vastness and intricacy of the natural world. She paused often to take in the breathtaking views, allowing herself to be fully immersed in the beauty that surrounded her.

The towering mountains stood as ancient sentinels, their rugged peaks reaching towards the sky with an air of timeless majesty. She traced the lines of their craggy faces with her eyes, marveling at the way they seemed to touch the heavens themselves.

The cascading waterfalls, their waters tumbling over rocky cliffs with a thunderous roar, filled the air with a sense of raw power and vitality. Old Mother Wilderness stood at their base, feeling the mist upon her face and listening to the symphony of sound as the water crashed against the rocks below.

And the lush valleys, with their verdant meadows and winding rivers, stretched out before her like a patchwork quilt of green and blue. She wandered through them with a sense of reverence, marveling at the abundance of life that thrived in their midst.

With each passing moment, she felt more connected to the land, more in tune with the rhythms of nature that sustained life in the wilderness. And though the journey ahead was filled with challenges and obstacles, she knew that she was exactly where she was meant to be – at home, in the heart of nature.

As she observed the wildlife around her, Old Mother Wilderness felt a deep sense of kinship with the creatures of the forest. She watched as the squirrels darted through the branches with agile grace, their bushy tails flicking behind them as they played amongst the leaves. The sight brought a smile to her face, reminding her of the simple joys that could be found in the wilderness.

The deer, with their elegant strides and attentive ears, moved through the forest with a quiet grace that captivated her. She admired their ability to navigate the dense undergrowth with ease, their movements a testament to their deep connection with the land.

And overhead, the birds circled and swooped with effortless grace, their wings slicing through the air with precision. Old Mother Wilderness marveled at their freedom, their ability to soar above the treetops and explore the vast expanse of the sky.

As Old Mother Wilderness continued her journey through the forest, she felt a deep sense of reverence for the land and all its inhabitants. With each step, she honored the ancient wisdom that permeated the very essence of the forest itself. She walked with a humility born of respect, mindful of her place as just one small part of a vast and intricate ecosystem that had thrived for millennia.

She listened to the whispers of the trees, their rustling leaves speaking a language older than time itself. She felt the pulse of the earth beneath her feet, a steady rhythm that connected her to the heartbeat of the land. And in the stillness of the forest, she heard the gentle murmurings of the spirits that dwelled within its depths, guiding her on her journey with unseen hands.

With each passing moment, Old Mother Wilderness felt more attuned to the natural world around her. She recognized herself not as an outsider, but as an integral thread woven into the intricate tapestry of life that spanned the forest. Every plant, every animal, every rock and stream was a vital part of the web of life, each contributing to the delicate balance that sustained the ecosystem as a whole.

And so, as she walked, Old Mother Wilderness offered prayers of gratitude to the spirits of the forest, honoring the plants and animals that sustained her on her journey. She gave thanks for the air she breathed, the water she drank, and the earth beneath her feet. For she knew that in the heart of the wilderness, every living thing was connected in a sacred dance of life and death, growth and decay.

As she continued her journey, Old Mother Wilderness carried with her the knowledge that she was never truly alone. For she was surrounded by the ancient wisdom of the forest, a timeless presence that guided her every step of the way. And though the path ahead was uncertain, she walked with a quiet confidence, knowing that she was exactly where she was meant to be – at home, in the heart of nature.

Amidst the trials and tribulations of her journey, Old Mother Wilderness encountered moments of unexpected beauty and wonder that filled her heart with awe and gratitude. In the midst of dense foliage and rugged terrain, she stumbled upon hidden glades carpeted with wildflowers, their vibrant colors painting the forest floor with hues of purple, yellow, and blue. The delicate petals swayed gently in the breeze, their sweet fragrance filling the air and uplifting her spirits during adversity.

As she traversed the wilderness, she stumbled upon hidden springs bubbling up from the earth, their crystal-clear waters flowing gracefully over smooth stones and moss-covered banks. The sound of their gentle babbling brought a sense of serenity to her soul, washing away the fatigue of her journey and refreshing her spirit with each cool, invigorating sip.

And as she ventured deeper into the heart of the forest, she stumbled upon hidden caves filled with ancient rock formations, their jagged edges and intricate patterns bearing witness to the passage of time. Within these caverns, she discovered the echoes of ancient civilizations, their presence felt in the faint etchings on the walls and the remnants of long-forgotten artifacts scattered across the floor. Each discovery filled her with a sense of wonder and reverence, a reminder of the rich tapestry of history that lay woven into the very fabric of the natural world.

In these moments of unexpected beauty and wonder, Old Mother Wilderness found solace and inspiration amidst the challenges of her journey. They served as reminders of the boundless beauty and diversity of the natural world, igniting a sense of awe and gratitude within her for the myriad wonders that surrounded her. And though the path ahead was fraught with uncertainty, she drew strength from these moments, knowing that they were a testament to the resilience and majesty of the wilderness that she called home.

In the tranquil embrace of the wilderness, Old Mother Wilderness found solace and contentment, embracing the solitude that surrounded her with open arms. Amidst the towering trees and the gentle rustle of leaves, she felt a sense of peace wash over her, soothing her spirit and calming her mind.

She reveled in the simple pleasures of life in the wild, finding joy in the warmth of the sun as its golden rays filtered through the canopy above, casting dappled patterns of light upon the forest floor. The gentle caress of the breeze against her skin brought a sense of refreshment, carrying with it the scent of pine needles and earth, mingled with the sweet fragrance of wildflowers in bloom. And as she walked beneath the shade of the trees, she felt a deep connection to the natural world around her, as though she were an integral part of the intricate tapestry of life that spanned the forest.

In these moments of solitude, Old Mother Wilderness found clarity and renewal, her senses heightened by the absence of human noise and distraction. She listened to the symphony of nature that surrounded her – the melodious chirping of birds, the soft rustle of leaves, the distant murmur of a nearby stream – and felt a profound sense of gratitude for the beauty and wonder of the world in which she lived.

And though the wilderness could be unforgiving at times, with its harsh weather and rugged terrain, Old Mother Wilderness found strength and resilience in the quiet beauty that surrounded her. For in the heart of the wilderness, where every moment was a testament to the power and majesty of nature, she knew that she was exactly where she was meant to be – at home, in the embrace of the wild.

With each step she took, Old Mother Wilderness carried with her a deep reverence for the land and all its inhabitants. She walked with a quiet humility, acknowledging her place as just one small part of a vast and intricate ecosystem that had existed long before her and would continue to thrive long after she was gone.

As she journeyed through the wilderness, she offered prayers of gratitude to the spirits of the forest, expressing her appreciation for the abundance of life that surrounded her. She honored the plants and animals that sustained her on her journey, recognizing their vital role in maintaining the delicate balance of the natural world.

In the presence of ancient trees and moss-covered rocks, Old Mother Wilderness felt a sense of connection to something greater than herself. She felt the spirits of the forest watching over her, guiding her footsteps, and filling her heart with a profound sense of peace and belonging. And though she walked alone, she knew that she was never truly alone, for she was surrounded by the unseen forces of nature that bound the world together in a web of life and energy.

With each prayer she offered and each step she took, Old Mother Wilderness deepened her connection to the land and its inhabitants, finding strength and solace in the knowledge that she was a part of something far greater than herself. And as she continued her journey through the wilderness, she carried with her the wisdom and guidance of the spirits, knowing that they would be her constant companions on the path ahead.

In the midst of her journey through the wilderness, Old Mother Wilderness paused to marvel at the breathtaking beauty and intricate complexity of the natural world surrounding her. She found herself captivated by the grandeur of towering mountains that reached towards the sky, their peaks cloaked in wisps of cloud and crowned with eternal snow. Each jagged ridge and craggy summit seemed to tell a story of the earth's ancient past, a testament to the immense power and enduring resilience of the natural forces that had shaped them over countless millennia.

As she gazed upon the rugged landscape, Old Mother Wilderness felt a deep sense of awe and reverence wash over her. She marveled at the majestic waterfalls that cascaded down sheer cliffs, their crystalline waters sparkling in the sunlight as they plunged into mist-shrouded pools below. The sound of rushing water echoed through the valleys, a symphony of nature's own creation that filled her heart with wonder and delight.

But it was not just the grandeur of the mountains and waterfalls that stirred her soul. Old Mother Wilderness found equal beauty in the serene tranquility of lush valleys, where emerald meadows stretched out as far as the eye could see, dotted with colorful wildflowers, and bathed in the golden light of the sun. The air was alive with the gentle hum of insects and the sweet melody of songbirds, creating a sense of harmony and peace that enveloped her like a warm embrace.

In the presence of such natural splendor, Old Mother Wilderness felt a profound sense of gratitude and humility. She recognized the delicate balance that sustained life in the wilderness, the intricate web of interconnectedness that linked every living creature to the land and to each other. And as she stood amidst the awe-inspiring beauty of the natural world, she knew that she was but a small part of something much greater – a timeless tapestry of life and energy that stretched across the earth and bound all living things together in a shared journey of existence.

Old Mother Wilderness moved through the forest with a sense of kinship and reverence for the creatures that inhabited its depths. She watched with fascination as squirrels darted among the branches, their bushy tails flicking back and forth as they played chase amidst the dappled sunlight filtering through the canopy above. Their nimble movements and playful antics brought a smile to her lips, reminding her of the joy and exuberance that could be found in the simple pleasures of life.

As she ventured further into the heart of the forest, Old Mother Wilderness encountered deer grazing peacefully in sun-dappled clearings, their graceful forms blending seamlessly with the natural beauty of their surroundings. She marveled at the elegance of their movements, the fluidity of their strides as they moved with effortless grace through the undergrowth. In their gentle demeanor and watchful eyes, she saw a reflection of her own connection to the land – a shared bond that transcended the boundaries of species and spoke to the universal language of the wilderness.

Above her, the sky was alive with the sound of birdsong as feathered inhabitants of the forest flitted from branch to branch, their vibrant plumage flashing in the sunlight as they danced through the air. Old Mother Wilderness listened to their melodic calls with a sense of wonder, each chirp and trill a testament to the beauty and diversity of life in the wild. She felt a sense of gratitude for the presence of these winged creatures, whose songs filled the forest with music and whose flights added color and movement to the ever-changing tapestry of the natural world.

As she observed the creatures of the forest going about their daily lives, Old Mother Wilderness felt a deep sense of connection to the intricate web of life that surrounded her. In their movements and behaviors, she saw echoes of her own existence – a reminder that she was not separate from the wilderness, but an integral part of its fabric. And as she continued her journey through the heart of the forest, she carried with her a newfound appreciation for the beauty and diversity of the natural world, and a sense of gratitude for the companionship of its wild inhabitants.

In the heart of the forest, Old Mother Wilderness breathed in deeply, savoring the crisp, clean air that filled her lungs. With each inhale, she felt a sense of renewal, as though the very essence of the forest infused her being with vitality and strength. The gentle rustle of leaves in the breeze whispered secrets of the ancient trees, their wisdom carried on the wind like a timeless melody.

Surrounded by the towering sentinels of the forest, Old Mother Wilderness felt a profound sense of peace settle over her. Here, amidst the age-old guardians of the land, she found solace and serenity, a sanctuary from the chaos and noise of the outside world. The rhythmic cadence of her footsteps echoed against the forest floor, a soothing lullaby that lulled her into a state of tranquility.

She walked along the winding paths that meandered through the forest, her senses alive to the sights and sounds around her. Sunlight filtered through the dense canopy above, casting dappled patterns of light and shadow upon the forest floor. The earthy scent of moss and decaying leaves mingled with the sweet fragrance of wildflowers, creating a symphony of aromas that filled the air with the essence of the wilderness.

As she walked, Old Mother Wilderness felt a deep connection to the land beneath her feet, to the ancient spirits that dwelled within its depths. She felt the pulse of life all around her, in the whisper of the wind through the branches, in the babbling of nearby streams, in the songs of birds echoing through the trees. In this moment, she was not just a wanderer in the forest – she was a part of it, woven into the very fabric of its existence.

AS OLD MOTHER WILDERNESS journeyed deeper into the heart of the forest, she stumbled upon hidden wonders that took her breath away. She stood in awe as she beheld hidden waterfalls cascading down sheer cliffs, their crystalline waters sparkling in the dappled sunlight that filtered through the canopy above. The sound of rushing water filled the air, a symphony of nature that resonated deep within her soul.

With each step she took, she discovered new marvels hidden within the depths of the forest. She stumbled upon hidden caves adorned with shimmering crystals, their facets catching the light and casting prismatic rainbows upon the walls. She marveled at the intricate formations that adorned the caverns, sculpted over millennia by the relentless force of water and time.

As she wandered further into the heart of the wilderness, she stumbled upon hidden meadows ablaze with a riot of wildflowers, their vibrant hues painting the landscape in shades of pink, purple, and gold. The air was alive with the hum of bees and the flutter of butterfly wings as they danced among the blossoms, pollinating the flowers and ensuring the continuation of life in the forest.

In the heart of the wilderness, Old Mother Wilderness underwent a profound metamorphosis. The raw, unbridled power of the forest permeated her very being, coursing through her veins like a primal force of nature. With each breath, she felt the wildness of the land infusing her, revitalizing her spirit and awakening her senses to the ancient rhythms of the earth.

Amidst the untamed beauty of nature, she discovered a deep sense of belonging that she had never known before. The towering trees, the rushing rivers, and the endless expanse of sky spoke to her in a language as old as time itself, whispering secrets of the land and revealing the hidden truths of the natural world. Here, amidst the symphony of life in the wilderness, she felt a profound connection to all living things, a sense of kinship that transcended the boundaries of species and echoed through the ages.

As the sun dipped below the horizon, casting a warm glow across the rugged landscape, Old Mother Wilderness stood amidst the towering trees, her senses alive to the sights and sounds of the forest. The soft rustle of leaves in the gentle breeze, the distant call of nocturnal creatures awakening to the night, and the ethereal dance of fireflies illuminating the darkness – all spoke to her in a language that transcended words.

With each passing moment, she felt a deep sense of peace settle over her, like a comforting blanket enveloping her weary soul. Here, in the heart of the wilderness, she found solace from the chaos of the world beyond, a sanctuary where she could reconnect with the primal rhythms of the earth and rediscover the true essence of her being.

As the first stars began to twinkle overhead, casting their soft light upon the forest floor, Old Mother Wilderness closed her eyes and whispered a silent prayer of thanks to the universe. For in this sacred place, amidst the untamed beauty of nature, she had found her home – a place of quiet contemplation, of boundless wonder, and of endless possibility. And as she stood beneath the canopy of stars, surrounded by the gentle embrace of the wilderness, she knew that she was exactly where she was meant to be – at peace, in the heart of the natural world.

# Reflections in the Stillness

Chapter 5

In the tranquil embrace of the wilderness, Old Mother Wilderness found solace in moments of quiet reflection. As she sat beneath the canopy of towering trees, surrounded by the gentle rustle of leaves and the melodic chirping of birds, she allowed her mind to wander.

Contemplating the passage of time, she marveled at how swiftly the years had flown by, like leaves carried away by the autumn breeze. Yet, in the stillness of the forest, she found clarity and perspective, understanding that time was but a fleeting illusion in the grand tapestry of existence.

With each passing moment, she felt a deeper connection to the rhythms of nature, a profound awareness of the interconnectedness of all living things. She watched as the sun traced its arc across the sky, casting shifting patterns of light and shadow upon the forest floor. She listened to the gentle murmur of the stream, the steady pulse of life that flowed through the heart of the wilderness.

In the quiet solitude of the forest, she found a sanctuary from the chaos of the outside world, a refuge where she could commune with the natural world and with her own innermost thoughts and feelings. Here, amidst the timeless beauty of nature, she found peace, serenity, and a sense of belonging that she had never known before.

As she sat in contemplation, she thought about the lessons learned and the wisdom gained over the years. She thought about the trials and tribulations she had faced, the moments of joy and sorrow that had shaped her journey. And though she had faced many challenges along the way, she realized that each one had been a stepping stone on the path to self-discovery and personal growth.

In the quiet stillness of the forest, she found the courage to confront her fears, the strength to overcome obstacles, and the resilience to persevere in the face of adversity. And as she reflected on her journey, she felt a sense of gratitude for the myriad experiences that had shaped her into the person she was today.

With each passing day, she grew more attuned to the whispers of her own heart and the guiding hand of fate. She embraced the uncertainty of the future, knowing that life was a journey of constant change and evolution. And as she sat in the embrace of the wilderness, she felt a deep sense of peace and contentment wash over her, knowing that she was exactly where she was meant to be.

In the tranquil solitude of the wilderness, Old Mother Wilderness delved deep into her memories, reflecting on the trials and tribulations that had punctuated her journey through life. She thought back to the moments of triumph and adversity, the victories and defeats that had shaped her into the resilient soul she had become.

Amidst the gentle rustle of leaves and the harmonious symphony of nature, she found solace and understanding. Each experience, whether joyful or sorrowful, had contributed to her growth and evolution. Every challenge had been a lesson, every setback an opportunity for introspection and renewal.

As she sat in quiet contemplation, she realized the profound interconnectedness of all things. The cycles of nature mirrored the ebb and flow of her own life, each season bringing its own lessons and revelations. Like the changing of the leaves and the shifting of the tides, she had embraced the inevitability of change, learning to flow with the currents rather than resist them.

In the stillness of the forest, she found clarity and purpose. She recognized that life was not a destination, but a journey—a journey of self-discovery, growth, and transformation. And though the path ahead remained uncertain, she embraced it with open arms, trusting in the wisdom of the universe to guide her every step of the way.

With each passing moment, she felt more attuned to the whispers of her own heart and the guiding hand of fate. She understood that true wisdom lay not in the pursuit of answers, but in the acceptance of the unknown. And as she surrendered to the flow of life, she found peace, contentment, and a deep sense of fulfillment in the beauty of the present moment.

Seated by the edge of a serene pond, Old Mother Wilderness found herself enveloped in the quiet majesty of nature. The stillness of the water mirrored the tranquility of her soul, reflecting the beauty of the surrounding landscape like a mirror to the heavens above. As she gazed into the depths of the pond, she contemplated the timeless rhythms of life—the cyclical patterns of birth, growth, decay, and renewal that echoed throughout the natural world.

With each passing moment, she felt a deep connection to the ebb and flow of existence. The ripples that danced across the surface of the pond were a poignant reminder of the transient nature of all things. Just as the water flowed inexorably onward, so too did life move forward in an eternal dance of creation and destruction.

In those moments of stillness, Old Mother Wilderness found solace and serenity. She recognized that life was a journey of constant change—a ceaseless cycle of beginnings and endings, of triumphs and tribulations. Yet, amidst the ever-shifting landscape of existence, there remained a timeless beauty—a beauty that transcended the limitations of time and space, a beauty that dwelled deep within the soul.

As she sat by the pond, immersed in the symphony of nature, Old Mother Wilderness embraced the impermanence of all things. She understood that change was not something to be feared or resisted, but rather embraced as an integral part of the human experience. For in the ever-changing tapestry of life, she found meaning, purpose, and a profound sense of peace.

In the timeless dance of the seasons, Old Mother Wilderness found herself an eager observer, attuned to the subtle changes that marked the passage of time. With each new dawn, she witnessed the awakening of the natural world—the tender buds of spring unfurling into vibrant blossoms, the lush foliage of summer basking in the warmth of the sun, the fiery palette of autumn painting the landscape in hues of red, orange, and gold, and the quiet stillness of winter blanketing the earth in a shroud of snow.

As she moved through the ever-changing landscape of the wilderness, Old Mother Wilderness marveled at the intricate tapestry of life that unfolded before her eyes. She saw the delicate balance between birth and death, growth and decay, creation and destruction—a testament to the eternal cycle of renewal that governed the natural world. In the fleeting beauty of a blooming flower, the majestic flight of a soaring eagle, and the gentle rustle of leaves in the wind, she found solace and meaning, knowing that each moment held within it the promise of new beginnings.

But amidst the grandeur of the natural world, Old Mother Wilderness also bore witness to the inevitable passing of time. She watched as the vibrant colors of summer faded into the muted tones of autumn, as the lush foliage withered and fell, and as the earth lay dormant beneath a blanket of snow. Yet, even in the depths of winter's embrace, she found beauty and resilience—a reminder that life, like nature itself, was a constant cycle of endings and beginnings.

In the rhythm of the seasons, Old Mother Wilderness found a source of comfort and reassurance. She understood that just as the earth would awaken from its winter slumber to greet the warmth of spring, so too would the human spirit rise from the depths of despair to embrace the promise of new life. And though the journey ahead was fraught with uncertainty, she took solace in the knowledge that each season brought with it the opportunity for growth, renewal, and transformation.

In the heart of winter, Old Mother Wilderness found herself drawn to the stark beauty of the frozen landscape. She ventured out into the snow-covered wilderness, her footsteps leaving behind a trail of imprints in the pristine powder. As she walked, she marveled at the silence that enveloped her—a profound stillness broken only by the occasional creaking of branches laden with snow and the soft whisper of the wind.

In the depths of the winter landscape, Old Mother Wilderness found solace and tranquility. She watched as the world around her seemed to come to a standstill, frozen in time beneath the icy grip of winter. Yet, amidst the seemingly lifeless landscape, she saw signs of resilience and renewal—the promise of life waiting to emerge from beneath the frost.

In the quiet beauty of the winter wilderness, Old Mother Wilderness found a sense of peace and renewal. She embraced the darkness of the season as a time for introspection and inner growth, a chance to reflect on the lessons learned and the wisdom gained. And though the days were short and the nights long, she took comfort in the knowledge that spring would soon come, bringing with it the promise of new beginnings and the warmth of the sun.

With the arrival of spring, the wilderness around Old Mother Wilderness underwent a remarkable transformation. The once barren landscape was now alive with the vibrant hues of new growth and the sweet fragrance of blossoms carried on the breeze. Everywhere she looked, she saw evidence of nature's resilience and renewal, a testament to the enduring cycle of life.

As she ventured out into the rejuvenated wilderness, Old Mother Wilderness felt a sense of wonder and awe wash over her. She watched as delicate buds unfurled into vibrant flowers, their petals reaching towards the sun in joyful celebration of the season's arrival. She listened to the melodious chirping of birds as they flitted from branch to branch, their songs filling the air with a symphony of sound.

In the midst of this newfound vitality, Old Mother Wilderness felt herself swept up in the energy of the season. The warmth of the sun on her skin infused her with a sense of rejuvenation and vitality, banishing the last traces of winter's chill from her bones. With each breath she took, she felt a renewed sense of purpose and belonging, as if the very essence of life itself flowed through her veins.

In the embrace of spring, Old Mother Wilderness found herself filled with hope and optimism for the future. She reveled in the beauty of the natural world, finding solace and inspiration in its boundless wonders. And as she walked through fields of wildflowers and listened to the joyful songs of birds, she knew that she was part of something greater than herself—a living, breathing tapestry of life, woven together by the threads of existence.

In the height of summer, when the sun hung high in the sky and the heat shimmered in waves over the land, Old Mother Wilderness sought solace in the cool embrace of the forest. As she wandered beneath the towering canopy of trees, she found relief from the oppressive heat, the dense foliage casting dappled shadows upon the forest floor.

In the quietude of the woods, she listened to the soothing symphony of nature—the gentle babble of a nearby stream, the rustle of leaves stirred by a gentle breeze, and the melodious chirping of crickets hidden in the underbrush. Each sound was a balm to her soul, offering a moment of respite from the clamor of the outside world.

As she walked, Old Mother Wilderness felt a sense of connection to the rhythms of the natural world. She marveled at the intricate dance of life unfolding around her—the vibrant hues of wildflowers carpeting the forest floor, the graceful flight of butterflies flitting from blossom to blossom, and the industrious buzz of bees as they went about their work.

As autumn approached, heralding the transition from the warmth of summer to the chill of winter, Old Mother Wilderness felt a subtle shift in the air. The days grew shorter, the nights cooler, and the forest transformed into a canvas ablaze with the fiery hues of fall.

As she wandered through the woods, she watched with a mixture of awe and melancholy as the leaves turned from vibrant greens to shades of red, orange, and gold. Each tree seemed to shed its summer cloak in a final burst of brilliance before succumbing to the inevitability of winter's grasp.

During this seasonal transformation, Old Mother Wilderness found herself reflecting on the cyclical nature of life. She understood that just as the trees shed their leaves in preparation for the harshness of winter, so too did humans undergo periods of shedding and renewal in their own lives.

Yet, amidst the melancholy of autumn's farewell, she also found beauty and solace. She marveled at the intricate patterns formed by fallen leaves on the forest floor, the crispness of the air that hinted at the promise of colder days ahead, and the melancholy beauty of the setting sun casting long shadows through the trees.

In the bittersweet embrace of autumn, Old Mother Wilderness found a sense of peace and acceptance. She understood that change was an inevitable part of life, and that each season brought with it its own gifts and challenges. And as she walked through the forest, surrounded by the sights, sounds, and smells of fall, she felt a profound gratitude for the beauty of the natural world and the preciousness of life itself.

In the tranquil embrace of the wilderness, where the boundaries between the physical and the spiritual seemed to blur, Old Mother Wilderness often found herself drawn into deep contemplation of the mysteries that lay beyond the realm of human comprehension. As she sat beneath the towering trees, their ancient branches reaching towards the heavens like outstretched fingers, she felt a profound sense of connection to the universe.

With each breath, she absorbed the symphony of nature—the gentle rustle of leaves, the distant call of birds, the murmuring of a nearby stream—and allowed herself to be enveloped by the sacred stillness of the forest. In these moments of quiet reflection, she felt as though she were communing with the very essence of existence itself.

She gazed up at the night sky, its vast expanse dotted with countless stars twinkling like distant beacons of light, and marveled at the sheer magnitude of the cosmos. She contemplated the mysteries of the universe—its origins, its infinite expanse, and the forces that governed its workings—and found herself humbled by the realization of her own insignificance in the grand scheme of things.

Yet, amidst the overwhelming vastness of the cosmos, Old Mother Wilderness also found solace in the interconnectedness of all living things. She understood that she was but a small part of a vast and intricate web of life, connected to every creature, every plant, and every rock and stream in the forest.

In the silence of the forest, she felt a sense of communion with something greater than herself—a divine presence that permeated every aspect of existence. She sensed the presence of the ancient spirits that dwelled within the trees, the rocks, and the waters, and felt as though they were guiding her on her journey through life.

Though she may never fully understand the mysteries of the universe, Old Mother Wilderness found comfort in the knowledge that she was a part of something infinitely larger than herself. She embraced the uncertainty of life with an open heart and a spirit of curiosity, knowing that every question posed, and every mystery explored brought her one step closer to the ultimate truth that lay at the heart of existence.

In the stillness of the night, with only the gentle rustle of leaves and the occasional hoot of an owl breaking the silence, Old Mother Wilderness found herself drawn to the heavens above. She lay back on the cool forest floor, cradled by the earth beneath her, and allowed her gaze to drift upwards towards the star-strewn sky.

As she beheld the vast expanse of the cosmos stretched out before her, Old Mother Wilderness felt a profound sense of wonder wash over her. Each twinkling star seemed to beckon her into the depths of space, inviting her to explore the mysteries that lay beyond the confines of her earthly existence.

She marveled at the sheer number of stars scattered across the celestial canvas, each one a distant sun, with its own retinue of planets and moons. Some stars burned brightly, casting their radiance across the cosmos, while others glimmered faintly, their light barely visible against the backdrop of darkness.

Old Mother Wilderness knew that each of these stars held a story—a tale of cosmic birth and death, of stellar evolution and cosmic cataclysm. Some had burned for billions of years, while others had flickered into existence only recently, their light still traveling across the vast expanse of space to reach her eyes.

In the face of such cosmic grandeur, Old Mother Wilderness felt a sense of humility and awe wash over her. She realized that her own life was but a tiny speck in the grand sweep of cosmic history, a fleeting moment in the vastness of time and space. And yet, paradoxically, she also felt a deep sense of connection to the infinite expanse of the universe, as though every atom of her being were intricately woven into the fabric of cosmic existence.

As the darkness of night slowly gave way to the soft light of dawn, Old Mother Wilderness found herself ensconced in a moment of serene beauty. She sat perched upon a moss-covered rock, nestled amidst the towering trees, and watched as the world around her began to stir from its slumber.

The first faint light of morning painted the eastern horizon in hues of pink and gold, casting a warm and gentle glow over the tranquil landscape. The darkness receded, giving way to the soft colors of dawn as they danced across the sky like brushstrokes on a canvas.

Old Mother Wilderness felt a sense of reverence wash over her as she witnessed the unfolding spectacle of nature. The air was cool and crisp, carrying with it the earthy scent of the forest and the sweet fragrance of dew-kissed flowers. She listened intently as the birds greeted the new day with their joyful songs, their melodies mingling with the gentle rustle of leaves in the breeze.

In those precious moments before the sun breached the horizon, Old Mother Wilderness found herself immersed in a world of quiet beauty and stillness. It was a time of transition, when the veil between night and day was at its thinnest, and the natural world seemed to hold its breath in anticipation of the coming day.

As the first rays of sunlight kissed the tops of the trees, Old Mother Wilderness felt a profound sense of gratitude well up within her. She was grateful for the beauty that surrounded her, for the peace and tranquility of the wilderness, and for the simple joys of being alive.

Surrounded by the symphony of the natural world, Old Mother Wilderness felt a sense of peace wash over her weary soul. The soothing sounds of the forest enveloped her like a warm embrace, offering comfort and solace in moments of uncertainty.

She closed her eyes and allowed herself to be fully present in the moment, letting go of worries and cares as she immersed herself in the tranquility of nature. The gentle rustle of leaves overhead whispered secrets of the ancient trees, their wisdom spanning generations beyond count. The melodious songs of birds echoed through the air, a testament to the enduring beauty of life in the wilderness. And the rhythmic flow of water, whether from a babbling brook or a cascading waterfall, served as a soothing reminder of the eternal cycle of renewal and rebirth.

In the embrace of nature's healing embrace, Old Mother Wilderness found a sanctuary for her weary soul. Here, amidst the towering trees and lush greenery, she felt a profound sense of connection to something greater than herself. She was reminded that she was not alone, but rather a part of the intricate web of life that spanned the forest.

With each breath of fresh air and each moment of stillness, she felt herself being replenished and revitalized. The worries and stresses of the world melted away, replaced by a deep sense of peace and contentment. In nature's embrace, she found the strength to face whatever challenges lay ahead, knowing that she was supported by the enduring beauty and resilience of the natural world.

As Old Mother Wilderness sat in the stillness of the forest, she couldn't help but marvel at the intricate dance of life unfolding around her. She observed the interwoven tapestry of existence, where every living being played a vital role in the delicate balance of nature.

She watched as bees buzzed from flower to flower, pollinating plants and ensuring their continued growth and reproduction. Each tiny insect, with its seemingly insignificant actions, contributed to the flourishing of the ecosystem as a whole. And in turn, the flowers provided nectar for the bees, sustaining them in their own journey.

Similarly, she witnessed the symbiotic relationships between plants and animals. The towering trees provided shelter and sustenance for countless creatures, from birds nesting in their branches to squirrels foraging for nuts among their roots. In return, these animals dispersed seeds and fertilized the soil, aiding in the trees' growth and propagation.

Even the smallest organisms, like fungi and bacteria, played crucial roles in the ecosystem. Beneath the forest floor, intricate networks of mycelium connected trees, transferring nutrients and information between them. Meanwhile, bacteria in the soil broke down organic matter, releasing vital nutrients that nourished plants and fueled the cycle of life.

As Old Mother Wilderness contemplated these interconnected relationships, she felt a deep sense of awe and reverence for the natural world. She realized that every creature, no matter how small or seemingly insignificant, had a part to play in the grand symphony of life. And in this realization, she found a renewed appreciation for the beauty and complexity of the wilderness that surrounded her.

Surrounded by the tranquil beauty of the forest, Old Mother Wilderness found solace in the simple yet profound rhythm of nature. She closed her eyes and allowed herself to be enveloped by the gentle symphony of sounds that filled the air. The rustle of leaves overhead, the distant call of a bird, the soft trickle of a nearby stream – each sound seemed to harmonize with the beating of her own heart.

In this moment of stillness, she felt a deep connection to the world around her, as if she were a part of something much greater than herself. She sensed the pulse of life coursing through the earth beneath her feet, the energy of the forest thrumming in perfect harmony with her own being.

As she breathed in the cool, fresh air, she felt a sense of calm wash over her, washing away the worries and cares that had weighed heavy on her mind. In the embrace of nature, she found refuge from the chaos of the outside world, a sanctuary where she could be truly present, truly herself.

With each breath, she felt herself sinking deeper into the stillness of the moment, letting go of the past and the future, and simply allowing herself to be. And in this state of quiet surrender, she found peace –

a peace that transcended words, a peace that could only be felt in the depths of her soul.

As Old Mother Wilderness gazed up at the vast expanse of the night sky, she felt a profound sense of wonder and humility wash over her. The stars shimmered like diamonds against the velvet canvas of space, each one a beacon of light in the darkness, a reminder of the infinite expanse of the universe.

In the silence of the night, she felt a deep connection to the cosmos, a recognition of her own smallness in the face of such grandeur. Yet, paradoxically, she also felt a sense of belonging, as if the very atoms of her being were woven into the fabric of the universe itself.

As she sat beneath the canopy of stars, she pondered the mysteries of existence – the origins of the universe, the nature of consciousness, the meaning of life itself. And though she may never find answers to these age-old questions, she found comfort in the simple act of contemplation, in the act of seeking understanding amidst the vastness of the unknown.

In the fading light of day, Old Mother Wilderness felt a sense of peace settle over her. She knew that, no matter how small she may be in the grand scheme of things, her presence mattered. She was a part of the cosmic dance of life, a participant in the ongoing story of creation.

And as she closed her eyes and surrendered to the beauty of the night, she felt a deep sense of gratitude well up within her. Gratitude for the gift of life, for the beauty of the natural world, and for the opportunity to be a witness to the wonders of the universe.

# Encounters with the Unknown

Chapter 6

The changing seasons ushered in a new chapter in Old Mother Wilderness's solitary existence. With the arrival of each season, the rhythm of life in the wilderness evolved, bringing unexpected encounters with travelers from distant lands to her secluded cabin. These weary wanderers, weary from their own odysseys, sought refuge and solace in the sanctuary of her humble abode.

Initially cautious, Old Mother Wilderness hesitated to invite outsiders into her sacred space, fearing the disruption they might bring to her harmonious connection with nature. Yet, as she beheld the weary faces and heard the tales of their trials, her heart softened with empathy. Recognizing in them the same longing for warmth and sustenance that had once driven her own journey through the wilds, she extended a welcoming hand and opened her door to these weary travelers. Through the flickering light of her hearth, she offered them not only physical shelter but also the warmth of her companionship and the solace of her stories.

The travelers who crossed paths with Old Mother Wilderness hailed from diverse corners of the world, each bearing a unique story etched upon their weathered faces. Some were weary wanderers, their footsteps worn by the miles traveled and their spirits weighed down by the burdens of their journeys. Seeking respite from the relentless march of time and the rigors of the road, they stumbled upon her cabin like lost souls adrift in the vast expanse of the wilderness.

Others arrived with the restless spirit of adventurers, their eyes alight with the fire of discovery and their hearts set ablaze with the promise of new horizons. Drawn to the untamed beauty of the wilderness, they sought refuge in Old Mother Wilderness's humble abode, eager to rest their weary bodies and replenish their spirits before embarking on the next leg of their daring quests. Each traveler brought with them a piece of the outside world, a fragment of distant lands and far-off dreams, weaving a tapestry of tales that mirrored the rich diversity of human experience.

Old Mother Wilderness listened intently to the tales spun by the weary travelers, her heart swelling with compassion for the trials and tribulations they had faced on their respective journeys. As they gathered around her hearth, she offered them the warmth of her cabin and the nourishment of her humble fare, inviting them to rest their weary bodies and replenish their spirits in the sanctuary of the wilderness.

In return for her hospitality, the travelers shared the stories of their lives, their voices carrying echoes of distant lands and far-off adventures. They spoke of the trials and tribulations they had overcome, the joys and sorrows they had experienced, and the wisdom they had gleaned along the winding paths of their wanderings. With each word uttered, a piece of their souls was laid bare, their vulnerabilities and strengths interwoven into the fabric of their narratives.

Old Mother Wilderness listened with rapt attention, her keen ears attuned to the cadence of their voices and the echoes of their hearts. She absorbed their words like a sponge, savoring the richness of their experiences and the depth of their insights. In the exchange of stories and shared moments, she found solace and camaraderie, forging connections that transcended the boundaries of time and space.

As the sun dipped below the horizon and the embers of the fire cast a warm glow upon the faces of the gathered travelers, Old Mother Wilderness and her unexpected guests found solace and camaraderie in the shared tales of their respective adventures. With each passing evening, they gathered around the crackling fire, their voices rising and falling like the gentle rhythms of the forest, weaving a tapestry of stories that spanned the breadth of their experiences.

Amidst the flickering shadows and the dancing flames, the travelers regaled Old Mother Wilderness with tales of distant lands and far-off realms, each story more captivating than the last. They spoke of towering mountains cloaked in mist, ancient ruins shrouded in mystery, and untamed wildernesses teeming with life. They recounted encounters with mythical creatures and legendary beings, sharing accounts of bravery, resilience, and the enduring spirit of adventure.

As the fire crackled and popped, casting dancing shadows across the faces of the gathered travelers, each recounted their encounters with the unknown. Some spoke of distant lands and exotic cultures, describing mountains that scraped the sky and oceans that stretched to the horizon like vast, endless seas of blue. They painted vivid pictures with their words, transporting Old Mother Wilderness and their fellow listeners to far-off realms filled with wonders beyond imagination.

Others shared tales of encounters with strange creatures – mythical beasts that prowled the night, their glowing eyes haunting the darkness; spirits that danced in the moonlight, their ethereal forms shimmering in the night sky; and fae folk that flitted through the shadows, their laughter echoing through the forest like the tinkling of bells. With each story, Old Mother Wilderness felt her understanding of the world expand, realizing that the boundaries of reality were far more fluid than she had ever imagined.

As she listened to the tales of the travelers, she found herself captivated by the rich tapestry of experiences they wove. Each story was a glimpse into a world both familiar and foreign, a reminder of the boundless mysteries that lay beyond the borders of her forest home. And as the night wore on and the fire burned low, she felt a deep sense of gratitude for the opportunity to share in their adventures, knowing that their tales would linger in her heart long after they had departed.

As the travelers spoke, Old Mother Wilderness felt a stirring within her, a yearning to venture beyond the familiar confines of her forest sanctuary and explore the vast unknown that lay beyond. With each tale of adventure and discovery, her imagination took flight, painting vivid images of distant lands and hidden realms in her mind's eye.

She felt a sense of wonder and curiosity stirring within her, a longing to experience the wonders of the world firsthand and unravel its myriad mysteries. The stories of mythical creatures and mystical encounters fueled her imagination, igniting a desire to seek out the truth behind the legends and folklore that had captivated her since childhood.

Though she had spent a lifetime wandering the wilderness, Old Mother Wilderness realized that there was still so much left to discover – hidden realms waiting to be explored, ancient secrets longing to be unearthed. And as the travelers shared their tales of adventure, she felt her resolve strengthen, knowing that the call of the unknown was one she could no longer ignore.

Amidst the tranquility of the forest, bonds of friendship and camaraderie blossomed between Old Mother Wilderness and her unexpected guests. Together, they shared moments of laughter and tears, finding solace and companionship in each other's presence amidst the vast expanse of the wilderness.

As they gathered around the fire each evening, the flickering flames casting a warm glow upon their faces, they shared stories of their pasts, their dreams, and their hopes for the future. Old Mother Wilderness found herself opening to her guests in ways she never thought possible, sharing the wisdom and experiences gained from a lifetime spent in harmony with nature.

In their shared experiences, they found a sense of belonging and understanding that transcended the barriers of language and culture. They laughed together, cried together, and forged memories that would last a lifetime, united by their shared journey through the wilds.

And as the days turned into weeks, Old Mother Wilderness realized that her unexpected guests had become like family to her, kindred spirits bound together by the threads of fate and the magic of the wilderness.

United by their shared sense of adventure, Old Mother Wilderness and her newfound companions embarked on explorations deep into the heart of the forest. Together, they wandered through hidden glades and secret groves, venturing into realms untouched by the passage of time.

In their explorations, they discovered hidden treasures concealed within the depths of the wilderness – sparkling streams cascading down moss-covered rocks, ancient trees with roots that delved deep into the earth, and vibrant wildflowers that painted the forest floor in a riot of colors.

As they marveled at the beauty of nature surrounding them, they gained a deeper appreciation for the delicate balance that sustained life within the forest. They observed the intricate dance of predator and prey, the symbiotic relationships between plants and animals, and the constant cycle of life and death that played out in every corner of the wilderness.

With each step they took, they felt more connected to the natural world, more attuned to the rhythms of the forest. And as they ventured deeper into the heart of the wilderness, they discovered a sense of wonder and awe that transcended language and culture, binding them together in a shared experience of the sublime.

As Old Mother Wilderness and her companions delved deeper into the heart of the forest, they encountered the untamed forces of nature that lay hidden within its depths. They weathered fierce storms that lashed the canopy above, their thunderous roars echoing through the trees like the voice of a wrathful deity.

Traversing treacherous terrain, they navigated steep cliffs and slippery slopes, their every step a test of strength and resilience. Yet, despite the challenges that lay in their path, they pressed onward, driven by a shared sense of determination and camaraderie.

In the shadows of the forest, they encountered wild beasts that prowled the underbrush, their eyes gleaming with primal instinct. They stood face to face with creatures both majestic and fearsome – from the silent prowling of wolves to the thunderous roar of bears. Yet, through courage and cunning, they navigated these encounters unscathed, earning a newfound respect for the creatures that called the wilderness home.

In the face of adversity, their bonds grew stronger, forged in the crucible of shared hardship. Together, they faced the challenges of the wilderness head-on, drawing strength from each other as they continued their journey into the unknown.

Old Mother Wilderness and her companions stood as a formidable force against the trials that beset them, their spirits fortified by the unyielding resilience of the wilderness that surrounded them. With each obstacle they encountered, they drew upon the bonds of friendship and the indomitable spirit of the forest to forge ahead.

As storms raged and winds howled through the trees, they stood steadfast, their resolve unshaken by the tempestuous fury of nature. They leaned on each other for support, finding strength in their shared determination to conquer the challenges that lay before them.

Through rugged terrain and perilous paths, they navigated with unwavering resolve, their footsteps echoing the tenacity of those who dared to tread where few ventured. They faced each trial with courage and perseverance, knowing that together they could overcome even the greatest of obstacles.

As the sun began its descent beyond the horizon, casting hues of orange and gold across the sky, the time came for the travelers to bid farewell to Old Mother Wilderness. Gathered around the flickering warmth of the fire one final time, they expressed their gratitude for her unwavering hospitality and the profound bond of friendship they had forged in the heart of the wilderness.

With heartfelt embraces and promises to meet again, they parted ways, each setting off on their own path, guided by the memories of their shared adventures and the lessons learned along the way. Though their journeys diverged, they carried with them the spirit of the wilderness and the enduring bonds of camaraderie that had been woven between them.

As they disappeared into the depths of the forest, their laughter and footsteps fading into the distance, Old Mother Wilderness watched with a sense of bittersweet nostalgia. Though their time together had been brief, the imprint they had left on her heart would remain forever etched in the fabric of her memories.

Alone once more amidst the quiet beauty of the wilderness, Old Mother Wilderness felt a sense of gratitude wash over her. She knew that the bonds of friendship forged in the crucible of shared experiences would endure, transcending the boundaries of time and distance. And as she gazed up at the twinkling stars overhead, she whispered a silent farewell to her dear companions, knowing that their paths would someday cross again.

As the echoes of their laughter faded and the forest once again embraced its solitude, Old Mother Wilderness found herself reflecting on the profound impact of her visitors' presence. Their brief sojourn in her humble abode had served as a poignant reminder of the interconnectedness of all living things and the boundless beauty that could be found in the most unexpected of encounters.

With a heart brimming with gratitude, Old Mother Wilderness resumed her solitary life amidst the tranquil embrace of the forest. Yet, the memories of her time spent with her unexpected guests lingered like a gentle breeze, weaving their way through the tapestry of her thoughts and infusing each moment with a newfound sense of appreciation for the simple joys of companionship and camaraderie.

As she wandered through the familiar paths of the forest, she found herself attuned to the subtle rhythms of nature, more aware than ever of the delicate dance of life unfolding around her. Every rustle of leaves, every whisper of the wind, carried with it the echoes of shared laughter and shared stories, a testament to the enduring bonds forged in the crucible of their time together.

In the quiet moments of solitude, Old Mother Wilderness found solace in the memories of their fleeting but profound connection. Their visit had left an indelible mark on her soul, a reminder of the richness and depth of human experience that transcended the boundaries of time and space.

With the passage of time, the memories of those encounters with the unknown remained ever-present in Old Mother Wilderness's mind. Like cherished treasures tucked away in the depths of her heart, she often found herself revisiting the moments shared with the travelers who had graced her humble abode, their stories weaving a tapestry of remembrance that colored the fabric of her solitary existence.

In the quiet moments of reflection, as she sat beneath the canopy of trees or wandered along the winding paths of the forest, Old Mother Wilderness would recall the faces of those who had journeyed to her doorstep seeking refuge and solace. Their laughter, their tears, and the wisdom they had imparted lingered in the air like a melody, a gentle reminder of the profound impact of their fleeting presence in her life.

Each memory was a thread in the rich tapestry of her experiences, a testament to the interconnectedness of all living beings and the enduring power of human connection. Though the travelers had long since departed, their essence remained intertwined with the fabric of her being, shaping the way she viewed the world and the depth of her understanding of the human spirit.

As the seasons continued to change and the years slipped by like grains of sand through an hourglass, Old Mother Wilderness found comfort in the knowledge that their time together, though brief, had left an indelible mark on her soul. Their stories had become a part of her own, interwoven with the rhythms of the forest and the eternal cycle of life and death.

And so, she carried their memories with her as she journeyed through the wilderness, a silent tribute to the enduring legacy of those chance encounters with the unknown. For in those moments of connection, amidst the vastness of the natural world, Old Mother Wilderness had discovered the true richness of life – the shared experiences, the bonds of friendship, and the timeless wisdom passed down from one traveler to the next.

As Old Mother Wilderness continued to dwell in her cherished forest sanctuary, she found herself enriched by the lessons and experiences garnered from those chance encounters with the outside world. The stories shared by the travelers had served as windows into realms beyond her own, expanding her understanding of the boundless diversity and complexity of existence.

In the quiet moments of solitude, as she communed with the ancient trees and listened to the whispers of the wind, Old Mother Wilderness reflected on the profound impact those encounters had left upon her. They had broadened her perspective, illuminating pathways of thought and understanding that stretched far beyond the confines of her woodland abode.

With each tale shared around the flickering flames of her hearth, she had gleaned insights into the myriad facets of human experience – the triumphs and tribulations, the joys and sorrows, the hopes and fears that bound all souls together in the intricate tapestry of life. Through the eyes of her transient guests, she had glimpsed the diverse landscapes, cultures, and creatures that inhabited the vast expanse of the world beyond her forest sanctuary.

Yet, even as she absorbed the richness of these newfound perspectives, Old Mother Wilderness remained steadfast in her connection to the land that had nurtured her from birth. For while the travelers had ignited a spark of curiosity within her, drawing her gaze toward the distant horizons and unexplored territories, her roots run deep in the soil of her beloved forest, anchoring her to the ancient rhythms of nature.

And so, she embraced the duality of her existence – rooted in the timeless wisdom of the wilderness, yet open to the ever-unfolding mysteries of the wider world. With each passing day, she found herself enriched by the symbiotic relationship between her solitary life amidst the trees and the transient encounters with those who journeyed through her woodland realm.

For in the end, it was the synthesis of these experiences – the harmonious blending of solitude and companionship, of familiarity and exploration – that shaped the essence of Old Mother Wilderness's being, infusing her with a depth of understanding and a breadth of wisdom that transcended the boundaries of time and space.

In the depths of her woodland sanctuary, surrounded by the age-old sentinels of the forest, Old Mother Wilderness found solace in the understanding that her journey through life was not a solitary one. While she may have traversed her path alone at times, she was ever mindful of the echoes of those who had graced her life with their presence – the travelers who had stumbled upon her humble abode, seeking shelter and sustenance amidst their own journeys.

Their memories lingered like faint whispers in the breeze, weaving themselves into the fabric of her being and intertwining with the ancient rhythms of the forest. Each encounter had left an indelible mark upon her soul, enriching her existence with the depth of human connection and the breadth of shared experience.

As she walked the familiar paths of her woodland realm, Old Mother Wilderness carried within her the stories and lessons gleaned from those transient guests. Their voices echoed in the rustle of leaves overhead, their laughter danced upon the dappled sunlight filtering through the canopy, and their footsteps reverberated in the soft earth beneath her feet.

In their tales of distant lands and exotic cultures, she found a mirror reflecting the infinite diversity and complexity of the world beyond her forest sanctuary. Through their eyes, she glimpsed the myriad wonders and mysteries that lay beyond the horizon, expanding her understanding of the boundless tapestry of existence.

And yet, even as she embraced the richness of these newfound perspectives, Old Mother Wilderness remained rooted in the timeless wisdom of her woodland home. For in the interconnectedness of all living things – from the towering trees to the smallest creatures of the forest – she found kinship and communion with the world around her.

# The Legacy of Old Mother Wilderness

Chapter 7

As the forest settled into the hush of evening, Old Mother Wilderness found herself enveloped in the tranquility of the fading light. The rustle of leaves in the gentle breeze and the distant calls of nocturnal creatures provided a soothing backdrop to her contemplation. With each passing moment, the sky transformed into a canvas of deepening hues, a silent reminder of the passage of time.

Sitting amidst the ancient trees, their gnarled roots intertwined with the earth beneath her, Old Mother Wilderness reflected on the journey that had led her to this moment. Her eyes, weathered by years of witnessing the cycles of nature, gazed out into the gathering darkness, searching for answers in the shifting patterns of light and shadow.

In the solitude of her forest sanctuary, Old Mother Wilderness recognized the profound impact she had made on those who had ventured into her realm. Though her days had been spent in quiet contemplation, her wisdom had rippled outward like the gentle currents of a stream, touching the hearts and minds of all who sought solace in the embrace of nature.

She recalled the countless travelers who had stumbled upon her humble abode, seeking refuge and sustenance amidst the wilderness. With each visitor, she had shared not only the warmth of her hearth but also the depth of her knowledge, offering guidance and insight gleaned from a lifetime of communion with the natural world.

As the fire crackled and danced in the hearth, casting flickering shadows upon the walls of her rustic dwelling, Old Mother Wilderness reflected on the countless conversations she had shared with her guests.

Their stories, woven together like the intricate threads of a tapestry, painted a vivid portrait of the human experience – a testament to the interconnectedness of all living things in the vast web of existence.

Beneath the towering sentinels of the forest, Old Mother Wilderness felt the weight of her years settle around her like a comforting cloak. Each gnarled trunk, each rustling leaf, whispered secrets of ages past, weaving a tapestry of memories that stretched back through the annals of time.

In the dappled light filtering through the canopy, she found solace and sanctuary, a refuge from the cares and worries of the world beyond. Here, amidst the ancient trees and murmuring streams, she had forged a life of purpose and meaning, rooted in the rhythms of the natural world.

As the gentle breeze stirred the leaves overhead and the scent of earth and pine filled the air, Old Mother Wilderness bowed her head in silent reverence. For in that moment, she knew that her legacy was not measured in deeds or accomplishments, but in the simple act of living in harmony with the land she loved.

In the heart of the forest, amidst the rustle of leaves and the gentle hum of insects, Old Mother Wilderness had discovered the true essence of existence. She had learned to listen to the whispers of the wind, to watch for the subtle signs of change in the natural world, and to find meaning in the simplest of moments.

For her, life was not a series of grand adventures or lofty ambitions, but rather a quiet journey of discovery and connection. Each day brought new revelations, new wonders to behold, as she wandered the paths of her beloved wilderness, attuned to its ever-changing rhythms.

And though she had lived a life of solitude, she had never felt alone. The forest was her companion, her confidante, her home. Its secrets were hers to uncover, its mysteries hers to ponder, and its beauty hers to cherish for all eternity.

And now, as she approached the twilight of her years, she found herself reflecting on the legacy she would leave behind. She knew that her time in this world was drawing to a close, but she also knew that her spirit would forever linger in the heart of the wilderness she had called home for so many years.

Her legacy was not one of grand monuments or tangible riches but rather of wisdom, kindness, and a deep reverence for the natural world. It was the stories she had shared around the campfire, the lessons she had imparted to those who sought her counsel, and the seeds of curiosity and wonder she had planted in the hearts of all who had known her.

As she gazed out at the forest that had been her constant companion, she felt a profound sense of peace knowing that she had lived a life true to herself and to the land she loved. And though her physical form would one day return to the earth, her spirit would forever soar among the trees, carried on the gentle breeze and woven into the fabric of the wilderness itself.

For Old Mother Wilderness, the legacy she left behind was not one of grand monuments or towering achievements, but rather one of quiet wisdom and enduring love. She had nurtured the land and its inhabitants with care and compassion, tending to the needs of the forest with a gentle hand and an open heart.

Her legacy was the songs of the birds that echoed through the trees, the babbling of the brooks that danced over rocks, and the rustle of leaves in the gentle breeze. It was the delicate balance of the ecosystem she had protected and the countless lives she had touched with her kindness and wisdom.

As she sat beneath the stars, enveloped by the comforting embrace of the forest, Old Mother Wilderness knew that her legacy would live on long after she was gone. It would be carried in the hearts of those who had known her and in the whispers of the wind that danced through the trees, a testament to the enduring power of love and stewardship for the natural world.

Her legacy lay in the lessons she had imparted to those who had crossed her path – the travelers who had stumbled upon her humble abode, seeking shelter and sustenance amidst their own journeys. Through her words and actions, she had shown them the beauty and wonder of the natural world, inspiring them to cherish and protect the wilderness for generations to come.

Old Mother Wilderness had taught them to listen to the whispers of the wind, to watch for the subtle signs of change in the natural world, and to find meaning in the simplest of moments. She had instilled in them a deep reverence for the land and its inhabitants, encouraging them to tread lightly upon the earth and to live in harmony with all living things.

And though her time in this world was drawing to a close, she knew that her legacy would endure in the hearts and minds of those she had touched. It would be carried forward by each traveler who had been inspired by her wisdom, each soul who had found solace in the quiet beauty of the wilderness she called home.

As she sat beneath the star-strewn sky, her eyes alight with the flickering flames of the campfire, Old Mother Wilderness felt a sense of peace wash over her. She knew that her time in this world was coming to an end, but she also knew that her spirit would live on in the whisper of the wind through the trees and the babbling of the brooks that meandered through the forest.

In that moment, surrounded by the timeless beauty of the wilderness she had called home, she felt a profound connection to the natural world and to all living things. She knew that her legacy would endure, not in monuments or grand gestures, but in the quiet moments of wonder and awe that she had shared with those who had walked alongside her on the journey of life.

For Old Mother Wilderness, the true measure of a life well-lived lay not in the accumulation of wealth or power, but in the impact one had on the world around them. And in that regard, she knew that her legacy would endure long after she was gone, woven into the very fabric of the wilderness she had called home.

Her teachings would echo through the generations, passed down from one steward of the land to the next, ensuring that the wisdom she had gained from a lifetime spent in communion with nature would continue to guide and inspire future guardians of the forest.

As she gazed up at the twinkling stars overhead, Old Mother Wilderness felt a sense of peace knowing that her life had not been lived in vain, but rather had left an indelible mark on the world around her.

As the night deepened and the stars shone brightly overhead, Old Mother Wilderness closed her eyes and let herself be carried away on the gentle currents of memory and reflection. She thought of the countless sunrises she had witnessed, the myriad creatures she had encountered, and the moments of quiet contemplation she had savored in the heart of the forest.

Each memory was a thread in the rich tapestry of her life, weaving together the moments of joy and sorrow, triumph and adversity, into a story that was uniquely her own. And as she drifted into the embrace of sleep, she carried with her the knowledge that her legacy would live on, written in the s of the wilderness she had loved so dearly.

And as she drifted into sleep, her dreams were filled with visions of the wilderness she had loved so dearly – its towering trees reaching towards the sky, its meandering streams glistening in the sunlight, and its inhabitants thriving in harmony with the land.

In her dreams, she wandered through the forest once more, feeling the soft moss beneath her feet and the gentle caress of the breeze against her skin. She listened to the symphony of nature – the chirping of birds, the rustle of leaves, the murmur of the brooks – and felt a profound sense of peace wash over her.

For in the realm of dreams, there were no boundaries or limitations, no barriers between herself and the natural world she cherished. And as she wandered deeper into the heart of the wilderness, she knew that her legacy would live on, etched into the very fabric of the land she had called home.

For Old Mother Wilderness, the legacy she left behind was not just a memory or a name carved into the annals of history, but rather a living, breathing testament to the enduring power of nature and the human spirit. It was a legacy of love, compassion, and reverence for the world around us – a legacy that would continue to inspire and uplift all who walked in her footsteps.

As the stars faded from the sky and the first light of dawn painted the horizon in hues of pink and gold, Old Mother Wilderness awoke from her dreams with a renewed sense of purpose. She knew that her time in this world was drawing to a close, but she also knew that her legacy would endure, carried forth by those who had been touched by her wisdom and kindness.

With a smile on her weathered face, she rose to greet the new day, ready to embrace whatever adventures lay ahead. For though her journey through life may have reached its end, the legacy of Old Mother Wilderness would live on, woven into the very fabric of the wilderness she had loved so dearly.

And so, as the first light of dawn began to creep over the horizon, Old Mother Wilderness opened her eyes to greet the new day. Though her journey through this world was coming to an end, she knew that her spirit would live on in the hearts of all who had been touched by her presence.

As she emerged from her humble abode into the crisp morning air, she felt a sense of peace wash over her. The forest whispered its secrets to her, the birds sang their morning songs, and the gentle babble of the nearby stream filled her with a profound sense of gratitude for the beauty of the natural world.

With each step she took, Old Mother Wilderness felt a deep connection to the land she had called home for so many years. She knew that her legacy would endure, carried forth by the countless creatures of the forest and the endless cycles of life and death that sustained the wilderness.

And so, with a heart full of love and gratitude, she embraced the new day, ready to continue her journey into the unknown with courage and grace. For though her time in this world may have been brief, the legacy of Old Mother Wilderness would live on, a beacon of hope and inspiration for all who followed in her footsteps.

In the quiet moments before dawn, as the world stirred from its slumber and the birds began to sing their morning songs, Old Mother Wilderness felt a sense of peace wash over her. She knew that her time in this world had been well spent, and that her legacy would endure for generations to come.

Sitting beneath the canopy of stars that adorned the predawn sky, she reflected on the many lives she had touched and the countless memories she had forged in the heart of the wilderness. Each moment, each encounter, had shaped her journey in ways she could never have imagined, and she was grateful for every step of the path she had walked.

As the first light of dawn began to paint the horizon with hues of pink and gold, Old Mother Wilderness felt a profound sense of gratitude for the beauty of the natural world. The forest whispered its secrets to her, the trees swaying gently in the early morning breeze, and she knew that she was exactly where she was meant to be – at home, in the heart of nature.

With a contented sigh, she rose to her feet and greeted the new day with open arms. Though her time in this world may have been brief, she knew that her legacy would endure, carried forth by the winds of change and the timeless rhythm of the wilderness. And as she set forth into the dawn, she did so with a heart full of love and a spirit unbound by the constraints of time and space.

And as she watched the sun rise above the treetops, casting its golden light upon the forest below, Old Mother Wilderness smiled, her heart filled with gratitude for the life she had lived and the legacy she would leave behind. For in the end, she knew that she had truly lived – and loved – with all her heart.

With a sense of peace and contentment settling over her, she embraced the beauty of the moment, allowing it to wash away any lingering doubts or fears. For she had lived a life guided by the rhythms of nature, and in doing so, she had found a profound sense of purpose and fulfillment.

As the first rays of sunlight danced through the trees, Old Mother Wilderness closed her eyes and let herself be carried away on the gentle currents of gratitude and love. She knew that her time in this world was drawing to a close, but she also knew that her spirit would live on in the hearts of all who had been touched by her presence.

And so, as the forest came alive with the songs of birds and the rustle of leaves, Old Mother Wilderness stood tall, her spirit soaring high above the treetops. For she knew that her legacy would endure, woven into the very fabric of the wilderness she had called home for so many years.

With a final glance towards the horizon, she whispered a silent farewell to the world she had loved so dearly, knowing that her journey was far from over. And as she disappeared into the depths of the forest, her legacy lived on, carried forth by the winds of change and the eternal beauty of the natural world.

# A Journey Beyond

## Chapter 8

As the sun dipped below the horizon, casting the forest in hues of orange and gold, Old Mother Wilderness stood at the edge of the wilderness she had called home for so many years. She felt a bittersweet pang in her heart as she looked out at the familiar landscape one last time, knowing that her time in this place was drawing to a close.

With each passing moment, she could feel the pull of the unknown growing stronger, urging her to venture beyond the boundaries of the forest that had been her sanctuary for so long. And though the prospect of leaving behind the familiar was daunting, she also felt a sense of excitement stirring within her soul.

For Old Mother Wilderness understood that change was an inevitable part of life, and that to resist it was to deny the very essence of existence itself. And so, with a deep breath and a heart full of courage, she took her first step into the great unknown that lay ahead.

Old Mother Wilderness felt a sense of liberation wash over her. She embraced the vastness of the world around her, reveling in the freedom to roam wherever her heart desired.

With each step she took, she left behind the cares and worries of her former life, allowing herself to be fully present in the moment. She drank in the sights and sounds of the natural world, savoring the beauty of each new landscape she encountered.

Though she knew that the road ahead would be filled with challenges and uncertainties, she also knew that she was ready to face whatever lay in store. For she carried with her the wisdom of the wilderness, a deep-rooted strength that would guide her through even the darkest of times.

As Old Mother Wilderness journeyed further from the forest that had been her home for so long, she encountered new and unfamiliar landscapes. She traversed rugged mountains, crossed vast deserts, and navigated dense jungles, each one presenting its own set of challenges and rewards.

Yet amidst the unfamiliarity of her surroundings, she found solace in the knowledge that she was not alone. Along the way, she encountered fellow travelers who shared her spirit of adventure, forming bonds that transcended language and culture.

Together, they faced the trials and tribulations of the journey, supporting each other through moments of hardship and celebrating the moments of joy. And though they hailed from different corners of the world, they were united by a common bond – a love for the natural world and a desire to explore its wonders.

In the company of her fellow travelers, Old Mother Wilderness found strength and camaraderie that she had not known before. Together, they faced the unknown with courage and determination, pushing forward through the obstacles that lay in their path.

They laughed in the face of adversity, finding humor in the most unlikely of places, and they shared stories of their past adventures around the campfire at night. In those moments of connection, Old Mother Wilderness felt a sense of belonging that she had not felt in a long time.

For though she had spent much of her life in solitude, she now realized that true companionship could be found in the company of kindred spirits who shared her passion for exploration and discovery.

As the journey continued, Old Mother Wilderness found herself growing more attuned to the rhythms of the natural world. She learned to read the signs in the sky, to navigate by the stars, and to listen to the wisdom of the winds.

She marveled at the intricate beauty of the landscapes she encountered, from the snow-capped peaks of the mountains to the lush greenery of the rainforests. And with each passing day, she felt herself growing more connected to the earth and all its inhabitants.

In the embrace of nature, she found solace and inspiration, drawing strength from the untamed beauty that surrounded her. And though the road ahead was long and uncertain, she walked it with a sense of purpose and determination, knowing that she was exactly where she was meant to be.

As she journeyed deeper into the unknown, Old Mother Wilderness encountered challenges that tested her courage and resilience. She faced fierce storms that lashed at her with wind and rain, and she traversed treacherous terrain that threatened to swallow her whole.

But with each obstacle she overcame, she emerged stronger and more determined than before. She learned to trust in her own instincts and abilities, knowing that she possessed the strength and resilience to overcome whatever challenges came her way.

And though there were moments of doubt and uncertainty, she never wavered in her conviction that she was on the right path. For she knew that the journey itself was its own reward, and that every step forward brought her closer to the truth she sought.

In the silence of the wilderness, Old Mother Wilderness found clarity and perspective that had eluded her in the busyness of her former life. She learned to quiet the noise of the outside world and listen to the voice of her own heart, trusting in its guidance to lead her true.

She reflected on the lessons she had learned and the wisdom she had gained along the way, cherishing the moments of insight and revelation that had illuminated her path. And with each new discovery, she felt a sense of wonder and awe at the boundless mysteries of the universe.

For Old Mother Wilderness understood that the journey of self-discovery was an ongoing process, a continuous unfolding of the soul that would never truly reach its end. And though she may never uncover all the answers she sought, she found fulfillment in the seeking itself.

As she journeyed onward, Old Mother Wilderness encountered fellow travelers who shared her thirst for adventure and exploration. Together, they forged bonds of friendship and camaraderie that would last a lifetime, supporting each other through the trials and tribulations of the journey.

They laughed together in moments of joy, finding solace in each other's company amidst the vastness of the wilderness. And when the road grew long and weary, they lifted each other up, reminding one another of the beauty and wonder that awaited them at the journey's end.

For Old Mother Wilderness, the companionship of her fellow travelers was a source of strength and inspiration that fueled her spirit and kept her moving forward, even when the path ahead seemed uncertain.

As the days turned into weeks and the weeks turned into months, Old Mother Wilderness found herself drawing ever closer to the destination she had set out to find. With each step forward, she felt a sense of anticipation building within her, a longing to finally uncover the truth she had been seeking.

And though the road ahead was fraught with challenges and obstacles, she pressed on with unwavering determination, knowing that she was on the brink of a discovery that would change her life forever.

For Old Mother Wilderness understood that the journey itself was as important as the destination, and that every twist and turn in the road had led her to this moment. And as she neared the end of her journey, she felt a sense of gratitude wash over her for the experiences she had gained and the lessons she had learned along the way.

At long last, after many months of travel and exploration, Old Mother Wilderness arrived at the destination she had been seeking.

Before her stretched a vast expanse of untamed wilderness, teeming with life and pulsing with the rhythm of the earth.

As she stood on the threshold of this new world, she felt a sense of awe and wonder wash over her, knowing that she had finally arrived at the place she had been searching for. And though the journey had been long and arduous, she knew that every step had been worth it to reach this moment.

For Old Mother Wilderness, this new chapter represented a fresh beginning, a chance to start anew and forge a life in harmony with the land. And as she stepped forward into the unknown, she did so with a sense of peace and acceptance, knowing that her spirit would forever roam the vast expanse of the natural world, a testament to the enduring power of solitude and the beauty of a life lived in harmony with the earth.

In the heart of the wilderness, Old Mother Wilderness found solace and serenity amidst the towering trees and meandering streams. She reveled in the simplicity of life in the wild, finding joy in the warmth of the sun on her skin and the cool touch of the breeze.

She marveled at the beauty and diversity of the natural world, finding wonder in the delicate balance that sustained life in the wilderness. And as she walked through the forest, breathing in the crisp, clean air and listening to the gentle rustle of leaves, she felt a sense of belonging that she had never known before.

For Old Mother Wilderness, the wilderness was not just a place to live, but a part of who she was – a reflection of her own untamed spirit and boundless love for the earth.

In the tranquility of the wilderness, Old Mother Wilderness found healing for her weary soul. She listened to the soothing sounds of the forest, the gentle rustle of leaves, the melodious songs of birds, and the rhythmic flow of water.

She allowed herself to be fully present in the moment, to let go of the worries and cares of the world and simply be. And in that stillness, she found a sense of peace and contentment that filled her heart with gratitude.

For Old Mother Wilderness, the wilderness was not just a place of refuge, but a source of strength and renewal that sustained her through even the darkest of times.

As she journeyed through the wilderness, Old Mother Wilderness encountered a myriad of creatures that called the forest home. She watched in awe as deer bounded gracefully through the underbrush, squirrels darted playfully between the trees, and birds soared overhead on outstretched wings.

She marveled at the intricate web of life that connected every creature to one another, from the tiniest insect to the mightiest predator. And as she observed the delicate balance that sustained life in the wilderness, she felt a deep sense of reverence for the natural world and all its inhabitants.

For Old Mother Wilderness, every encounter with the creatures of the forest was a reminder of the interconnectedness of all living things, and of the beauty and wonder that could be found in the most unexpected of places.

In the twilight of her years, Old Mother Wilderness reflected on the legacy she would leave behind. Though she had lived a life of solitude, her presence had touched the lives of all who crossed her path. Her wisdom had inspired countless souls, and her spirit would forever linger in the heart of the wilderness she called home.

She knew that her time in this world was drawing to a close, but she also knew that her spirit would live on in the whisper of the wind through the trees and the babbling of the brooks that meandered through the forest.

For Old Mother Wilderness, the legacy she left behind was not one of grand monuments or towering achievements, but rather one of quiet wisdom and enduring love. She had nurtured the land and its inhabitants with care and compassion, tending to the needs of the forest with a gentle hand and an open heart.

Her legacy lay in the lessons she had imparted to those who had crossed her path – the travelers who had stumbled upon her humble abode, seeking shelter and sustenance amidst their own journeys. Through her words and actions, she had shown them the beauty and wonder of the natural world, inspiring them to cherish and protect the wilderness for generations to come.

As the final chapter of her story drew near, Old Mother Wilderness embraced the inevitability of change. With a sense of peace and acceptance, she bid farewell to the wilderness that had been her faithful companion for so long.

In her heart, she knew that her spirit would forever roam the vast expanse of the natural world, a testament to the enduring power of solitude and the beauty of a life lived in harmony with the earth.

Old Mother Wilderness felt a sense of liberation wash over her. She embraced the vastness of the world around her, reveling in the freedom to roam wherever her heart desired.

With each step she took, she left behind the cares and worries of her former life, allowing herself to be fully present in the moment. She drank in the sights and sounds of the natural world, savoring the beauty of each new landscape she encountered.

Though she knew that the road ahead would be filled with challenges and uncertainties, she also knew that she was ready to face whatever lay in store. For she carried with her the wisdom of the wilderness, a deep-rooted strength that would guide her through even the darkest of times.

And though there were moments of doubt and uncertainty, she never wavered in her conviction that she was on the right path. For she knew that the journey itself was its own reward, and that every step forward brought her closer to the truth she sought.

In the silence of the wilderness, Old Mother Wilderness found clarity and perspective that had eluded her in the busyness of her former life. She learned to quiet the noise of the outside world and listen to the voice of her own heart, trusting in its guidance to lead her true.

She reflected on the lessons she had learned and the wisdom she had gained along the way, cherishing the moments of insight and revelation that had illuminated her path. And with each new discovery, she felt a sense of wonder and awe at the boundless mysteries of the universe.

For Old Mother Wilderness, the journey beyond the familiar was not just an adventure, but a profound spiritual awakening. It was a chance to reconnect with the earth and all its inhabitants, to find her place in the vast tapestry of existence, and to embrace the beauty and wonder of the natural world in all its glory.

Epilogue

# The Eternal Wilderness

Chapter 9

In the years that followed Old Mother Wilderness's departure from the forest she had called home, her legend grew and evolved, taking on a life of its own in the hearts and minds of those who heard her story. From generation to generation, her name became synonymous with the wild places of the world, a symbol of strength, wisdom, and resilience in the face of adversity.

In the small villages and bustling cities that dotted the landscape, people spoke of Old Mother Wilderness with reverence and awe, passing down tales of her encounters with the unknown and her deep connection to the natural world. Her memory became enshrined in song and story, her image immortalized in paintings and sculptures that adorned temples and shrines dedicated to the wilderness she had loved so dearly.

But it was not just in the realm of mortal beings that Old Mother Wilderness's spirit lived on. In the depths of the forest she had called home, her presence lingered like a whisper on the wind, a gentle reminder of the power and majesty of the wild places of the world. The trees whispered secrets passed down through the ages, their branches reaching towards the sky in silent tribute to the woman who had once walked among them.

The animals, too, paid homage to Old Mother Wilderness, their songs and calls echoing through the forest in a chorus of gratitude and reverence. They knew that she had been a friend and protector of their home, and they honored her memory with every bound and leap, every rustle and chirp that filled the air.

As the seasons continued to turn and the years stretched on into eternity, the wilderness itself became a living testament to Old Mother Wilderness's legacy. The trees grew tall and strong, their roots delving deep into the earth, anchoring them to the land she had loved so dearly. The rivers flowed freely, their waters teeming with life, a reflection of the vibrant ecosystem she had nurtured with care and compassion.

And though the world beyond the forest continued to change and evolve, the wilderness remained a sanctuary of peace and tranquility, a haven for those who sought solace and renewal amidst the chaos of modern life. For in the heart of the wilderness, Old Mother Wilderness's spirit lived on, a timeless guardian of the land she had loved so dearly.

In the quiet moments before dawn, when the world lay still and silent, those who ventured into the depths of the forest could feel Old Mother Wilderness's presence all around them, a gentle whisper in the breeze, a flicker of light in the darkness. They knew that she watched over them with a mother's love, guiding them through the trials and tribulations of life with a steady hand and a kind heart.

And though her physical form had long since returned to the earth from which it had sprung, her spirit soared free, like a bird in flight, unbound by the constraints of time and space. For in the eternal wilderness, there was no beginning and no end, only the endless cycle of life and death, growth and decay, creation and destruction.

In the quiet moments before dawn, when the world lay still and silent, those who ventured into the depths of the forest could feel Old Mother Wilderness's presence all around them, a gentle whisper in the breeze, a flicker of light in the darkness. They knew that she watched over them with a mother's love, guiding them through the trials and tribulations of life with a steady hand and a kind heart.

And though her physical form had long since returned to the earth from which it had sprung, her spirit soared free, like a bird in flight, unbound by the constraints of time and space. For in the eternal wilderness, there was no beginning and no end, only the endless cycle of life and death, growth and decay, creation and destruction.

As the sun rose above the horizon, casting its golden light upon the forest below, the creatures of the wilderness stirred from their slumber, their voices raised in a chorus of greeting to the new day. And amidst the rustle of leaves and the gentle hum of insects, Old Mother Wilderness's spirit danced, weaving through the trees like a wisp of smoke on the wind.

For in the eternal wilderness, there was no separation between the physical and the spiritual, the material and the ethereal. All was one, bound together in a seamless tapestry of existence that stretched from the depths of the earth to the farthest reaches of the cosmos.

In the depths of the forest, where the light of the sun scarcely penetrated the dense canopy overhead, Old Mother Wilderness's spirit found solace and serenity, a refuge from the cares and worries of the mortal world. Here, amidst the towering trees and the cool, damp earth, she reveled in the timeless beauty of the wilderness, drinking in the sights and sounds of the natural world with a sense of wonder and awe.

For in the eternal wilderness, there was no need for words or explanations, no need for the trappings of human civilization. Here, in the heart of nature, everything was as it should be, perfect and whole, a testament to the inherent balance and harmony of the world.

And so, as the ages passed and the world continued to change, the eternal wilderness remained a constant, a beacon of hope and inspiration for all who sought solace and renewal amidst the chaos of the world. For in its depths lay the essence of Old Mother Wilderness's spirit, a guiding light for all who walked in her footsteps.

And though her physical form had long since returned to the earth, her legacy lived on in the hearts of those who cherished the wild places of the world. For in the eternal wilderness, she would forever be remembered as a guardian and protector, a symbol of the enduring power of nature and the human spirit.

In the twilight of the evening, as the stars began to twinkle overhead and the world grew quiet once more, Old Mother Wilderness's spirit watched over the forest like a silent sentinel, her presence a comforting presence in the darkness. And as the creatures of the night went about their business, she smiled, knowing that her legacy would endure for all eternity.

For in the eternal wilderness, there was no need for fear or doubt, no need for sorrow or regret. Here, in the heart of nature, all was as it should be, perfect and whole, a testament to the enduring power of love and the beauty of a life lived in harmony with the earth.

And so, as the final chapter of her story drew to a close, Old Mother Wilderness's spirit soared high above the treetops, a radiant beacon of light in the eternal wilderness. For though her physical form had long since departed, her legacy would live on forever, woven into the very fabric of the natural world she had loved so dearly.

And as the sun dipped below the horizon, casting the forest in hues of orange and gold, the creatures of the wilderness sang their songs of gratitude and reverence, their voices rising in a chorus of celebration for the life of Old Mother Wilderness, a guardian and protector of the wild places of the world.